Sacked So What

Vincent Ogutu

Address: P.O. Box 35072-00200, Nairobi, Kenya

Tel: +254 722 171 838

Email: ogutuvin@gmail.com

Copyright ©2017 by Vincent Ogutu

Printed and Bound in Kenya by:

CLC Kenya, Print On Demand

Hurlingham Park C2,

Argwings Kodhek Road.

P.O Box 26665 00100

Nairobi. Kenya.

Tel: +254 734 / 701 446729

Email: pod@cblafrica.com

www.clcinternational.org.

Cover design & layout by:

MediaGraphics Studio

Tel: +254708625252

Email: desgichuru@gmail.com

Unless otherwise stated, Scripture quotations are taken from the Holy Bible, *New International Version*

ISBN: 978-9966-107-20-6

Dedication

This book is dedicated to humanity, all the people struggling in life one way or another. There is hope. The Creator who made you, made you with all that you need. Seek Him and all (provisions) will be added (supplied) unto you. Discover how you can become a core creator for it is indeed in your capacity and your thoughts; there is no limitation to what you can do, achieve or become. Success in life comes from service to humanity. Identify your gifting and how you can use them to serve.

May this book inspire, give hope and minister to humanity for there is HOPE.

Acknowledgement

First and foremost, I thank the Almighty God for the vision and the inspiration to write, addressing the problem of job loss and means of coping with this undesired temporary situation.

Secondly, I acknowledge all persons who have contributed their real life stories to encourage persons who for one reason or another find themselves out of employment. Special thanks to Tsheena, Angela, Calisto, Joan, Sarah, Charles, Mercy, Maingi and Phyllis.

Thirdly, I recognize the push by readers who appreciated my first book "Life is Like That: Power of Life Contradictions" for their continued request for another book.

Lastly, I thank my dear family: Everlyne my dear wife and lovely daughter Ivana, for the support they offered me during the long hours of reflecting, reading and writing sessions. May your sacrifice give hope to the hopeless and give direction to those who feel stuck or lost. It is my prayer that no life should be lost to depression, drugs or violence; life is precious. There is HOPE.

Endorsements

"Vincent is a thought leader who is inclined to quick actions in any presenting situation. He is blunt and practical in his thoughts. As an alumnus of the Wealth Creation Masterclass, he has lived true to the creed of monetizing his competences and passions. This book is a testimony of the practical entrepreneur that Vincent is." – *Wahome Ngari,* **Financial Educator & CEO**

I have been inspired to focus on the goal no matter how treacherous the path is.
Jonah Kimani, **SEKU**

"In this book, Vincent aptly documents successful entrepreneurship journeys majorly emanating from people losing jobs or resigning. He presents a hope; that it is achievable." **– Verah Omwocha, Book editor and Writer**

"Once again, Vincent proves that Entrepreneurship is a journey worth taking. He believes that it is not over until it is over"**- Winnie Ogenche, Editor and Writer.**

Contents

Foreword

Vincent presents a book that will provoke a subject that is common in Kenya today. The workplace at present has a high labour turnover and HR consultants are equally busy recruiting new staff to fill places. This book truly seeks to speak into the life of those that are shown the door, leaving a huge question mark in their present life. Readers will find help in resolving the dilemma of separating from the organizations they have been working for. It is also a great reflection for those that forecast that one day they will exit formal employment and pursue individual goals.

The literature is done in a simple mastery way that makes reading easy and informative. Real case studies are applied to show how various individuals have dealt with their 'tragedy' to propel them to higher heights. One is left inspired and with an appetite to seek opportunities that are a splash in the world that we live in. It literally implores all that everyone can achieve greatness without exception.

You will find the script a great support in provoking the talent and skill set that is resident in your life that can be exploited excellently. The book will encourage and stimulate you to rethink your life purpose. One author said 'if you do not know where you are going, any road will lead you there'. The case studies have demonstrated how these people connected with their life calling and went out to achieve the most. Instead of dealing with generalities, they focused in an area of interest and give it their all.

The author has dedicated his time to coach entrepreneurs and I am most convinced that the book will go a long way to support those who continue to dream concerning ways to serve humanity in profound ways. I will encourage that the readers inspired by this work continue to seek like-minded people and business support so that consistency can be sustained.

Indeed this book will appeal to all who support those separating with firms, retirees and those of us in business development in need of inspiration and motivation to grow.

Joseph M. Mbugua,

Bsc, Mech, MA, Leadership, MBA

Entrepreneur and Business Mentor

Abbreviations

APC AspirinParacetamol Caffeine

BAT British American Tobacco

BNI Business Networks International

CD Compact Disc

CPS Certified Public Secretary

CUE Commission of University Education

CV Curriculum Vitae

DNA Deoxyribonucleic Acid

DRC Democratic Republic of Congo

DVD Digital Versatile Disc

EABL East African Breweries Limited

ECD Early Childhood Development

FMCG Fast Moving Consumer/household Goods

IATA International Air Transport Association

ICT Information Communication and Technology

IEA Institute of Economic Affairs

IT Information Technology

JKUAT Jomo Kenyatta University of Agriculture and Technology

KBA Kenya Bankers Association

KCISI Kenya Credit Information Sharing Initiative

KEBS Kenya Bureau of Standards

KEPSA Kenya Private Sector Alliance

KES Kenya Shillings

KNBS Kenya National Bureau of Statistics

KRA Kenya Revenue Authority

MNC Multinational Corporation

NGO Non - Governmental Organization

NWM Network Marketing

Sacco Savings and Credit Cooperative Organizations

SEDC Strathmore Entrepreneurship Development Centre

SEKU South Eastern Kenya University

SME Small and Medium Enterprises

TEEP Tony Elumelu Entrepreneurship Programme

TSC Teachers Service Commission

UAE United Arabs Emirates

UK United Kingdom

UNCTAD United Nations Conference on Trade and Development

UNHCR United Nations High
Commissioner for Refugees

USA United States of America

VIP Very Important Person

VSS Voluntary Severance Scheme

YWCA Young Women Christian
Association

Glossary

Ardhi - a Swahili word meaning land

Askari's - County police who maintain law and order

Chama - investment groups used as social capital and insurance

Chaqula - Name of Business implying food

Gikomba - An open air market in Nairobi

Mabati - Tin structure made of iron sheets

Omekannya - One who is like the father, in Igbo (a Nigerian dialect in Eastern Nigeria)

Keep away from people who belittle your ambitions. Small people always do that, but the really great make you feel that you, too, can become great. –Mark Twain

Introduction

The world is an interesting stage, where we are all called to play our part and exit when done. People find themselves in different roles. This has happened since time immemorial. In history, we had masters and slaves. There was total submission to authority; deviance was unheard of. A little resistance led to extreme use of force. It is said that some rulers fed lions with living flesh at the slightest imagination of non-conformity.

As societies advanced, there was need for a balanced use of authority. We still had the rulers (leaders) and the led (masses) with some written law (read) constitution that guaranteed rights and responsibilities. There were owners of resources and labourers who worked for wages. The wages were just enough to cater for basic needs – to keep them away from starvation. Others claim that "a salary is a 'pain killer' that creates dependence."

From our common history, irrespective of race or continent, this story is familiar. You can recall Joseph the Prime Minister of Egypt with King Pharaoh and the cabinet on one side, and farmers, labourers, soldiers and slaves on the other. In many African communities there were community leaders: chiefs, kings and the council of elders or opinion shapers. The opinion shapers were seers, fortune tellers, herbalists or witchdoctors. They were believed to have mystical powers not well understood.

In the 21st century, this story has not changed much. The more it changes the more it remains the same. Today we not only have landlords but also entrepreneurs who create and control means of production or trade. This means that the entrepreneurs are the new "land-owners" and the employed are the labourers working in their establishments for a fixed wage (read salary); while the entrepreneurs enjoy profits and great wealth.

In the past, slaves were whipped mercilessly. Today, one is given a 'whipping letter' - dismissal letter. The dismissal can take many forms namely;

severance pay, interdiction, retrenchment, layoff, end of contract, forced retirement, resignation, outsourcing and renewable contracts among many other names. What is common and clear is that the contract between the employer and the employee is coming to an end. There is no job for you, period! In some cases one has the opportunity to sack their bosses.

This communication usually from the human resource department or immediate supervisors is not the most palatable. Those who have experienced this will attest to the difficulty of giving this letter, counselling an employee at the verge of losing the *mighty salary*.

If it has not happened to you, it may occur to you, prepare as you work. If it has happened, always have survival strategies to cushion you from extreme hardship. Truth be told, in today's economy with plenty of graduates looking for employment if you lose your job, it will take you 6-12 months before you get a suitable placement depending on your skills, experience, social and professional networks.

The business environment has not been favourable globally over the past few years. To understand what is happening locally we need to understand global data. The world population is believed to be approximately 7 billion people. Looking at the distribution of this population critically, we will discover that the seven billion is divided as follows: 400 million people are entrepreneurs, 430 million are unemployed, 577 million are over 64 years old hence too old to work, 1.9 billion are minors (0-15 years) either at home or in school, 1.7 billion people work in the service industries, 1.4 billion people work in the agricultural industry and lastly only about 800 million people work in the industrial outfits.

Data from United Nations Conference on Trade and Development (UNCTAD) estimates that the world will require over 600 million jobs over the next fifteen years. This has to be done to arrest negative impacts on society namely; extreme poverty, crime and starvation.

According to 2016 Kenya National Bureau of Statistics (KNBS), Kenya has a population of approximately 45.4 million people. Of this population, the employed population according to government statistics is about 16 million. The employed are in the informal sector commanding approximately 13.3 million people. The formal sector employs approximately 2.7 million people (public and private sector).

Looking at the Kenyan statistics further, one will discover that the private sector employs about 1.8 million people while the public sector employs about 737,100 people as estimated figures of 2016. The next question would be how employment is distributed in the public sector. Teachers' Service Commission (TSC) employs 297,000 (teachers and support staff), Ministries employ 180,600; parastatals 94,500; government corporations 45,400 and lastly county governments 118,900 workers approximately.

Examining the informal sector as a creator of jobs and employment, we discover that the Manufacturing sector contributes 2,710,200; Construction 337,100; Retail/ wholesale, hotels and restaurants 7,946,700; Transport and Communication contribute 417,200; community, social and personal service 1,293,400 and lastly other 605,100 employees. The urban-rural employment distribution is 4,709,900: 8,599,800 (KNBS, 2017)

Further exploration of available data in the economic survey (KNBS, 2017), shows that universities (both public and private) churn out approximately over 50,000 graduates yearly. In retrospect, this will be creating a job gap of over 9 million persons within the next ten years. Where will they get jobs? Unofficial unemployment stands at 40% for ages between 15- 35 according to Institute of Economic affairs (IEA). The number of university graduates stands at less than 1 million since independence according to Commission of University Education (CUE).

The business environment has been harsh due to globalization, increased competition and disruptions due to technological advancements. Banks, manufacturing firms and service driven organizations have not been spared. It is estimated that about 10,000 people lost their jobs according to Kenya Employers and private Sector Association (KEPSA) in the last two years.

The technology brings about efficiency and increased productivity with little role for manpower.

To enable one survive the unexpected job loss, people need to be encouraged to invest in personal development acquiring skills, experiences and networks. These networks are useful when your contract becomes redundant. Can one monetarize their skills effectively? Always invest in new knowledge and relationships as you look for opportunities.

The end of a contract takes several facets. There are reports that when you report to work you find the guards have been changed and there is no access to the working premises. All employees or a full department being called to a conference hall and you see new faces. With no smile on their faces they announce the business is being closed down or the services are being out-sourced. You are advised to collect your terminal dues from the finance office and you can re-apply to the new entity in-case you can be considered.

I happen to have experienced this first hand after completing my form four. I worked at a renowned bakery among the oldest in the Kenyan history. When we reported one morning, the operations had been halted, guards were new and a notice at the gate simply said "collect your dues from the finance office after 11am".

This book is about real life stories of people like you and me who have had a chance to undergo the baptism of "you are fired". The experience is excruciating and many would wish they would be shot dead. A gun would make it final. There is so much to life to give up so easily. *Sacked! So What*? This is a worthy companion one should have in case you find yourself on the receiving end. We can also learn from the stories of the brave ones who fired their bosses. It shares authentic life stories of how others overcome this temporary hiccup with great success beyond their expectation to others' amazement.

I've missed more than 9000 shots in my career. I've lost almost 300 games. Twenty-six times I've been trusted to take the game-winning shot and missed. I've failed over and over and over again in my life. And that is why I succeed.

- Michael Jordan, (American professional Basketball player & chairman of Charlotte Hornets

#1: *The Bombshell*

Your time is limited, so don't waste it living someone else's life. –Steve Jobs

Tell-tale signs

The drill is almost familiar. The work environment has routines we all get used to; regular meetings, emergency meetings and disciplinary meetings. There is always a tell-tale sign which we always ignore. When you start hearing rumours from your colleagues, and things are not getting any clearer, prepare for the unknown for most work environments have cartels (information sources) who share information. You may have been discussed in places outside the work environment, be grateful you are getting clues. The fall can be less painful and less of a surprise.

Responsibilities are not being delegated to you as before. Some meetings are happening which you need to be a part of; you are either not informed or simply ignored. If your boss was never friendly at all and all over sudden he or she is willing to offer you a cup of tea, know that your goose is cooked. When junior colleagues start looking at you whenever you approach and start giggling, things are getting elephant.

You are called for a meeting in the board room out of the blue. Wondering what is going on, you pick your diary and laptop as usual. There you meet a representative from the human resource department and your boss' boss. Your head races 'where is my immediate boss?' The first question is not friendly. "What is happening?" you are asked. The committee in your *head* is sweating, 'where? How? Who? What?' Then, prolonged silence follows.

The truth

The boss then declares that the department is experiencing difficulties sustaining the business. As a short term measure, roles will be combined and your department is going to be scrapped. Being a good employee, the company is willing to lessen your pain by giving you three month severance pay, pay all leave days not taken, pay gratuity for every year worked. You are not calculating the last cheque, in your mind you are asking yourself *'why me?' How I worked tirelessly for this organization, they are not even appreciating my input!* I submit to you they appreciated, that is why they paid you a monthly salary without fail.

The half an hour meeting seems like a full day. A letter is passed to you across the table and you are informed that you can talk to anyone in the organization to assist you with handover. You start thinking of what will happen to your junior staff now that the department is being scrapped. You rush to the washroom and lock yourself in this safe place, the letter crashed in your hands, you are trembling. Your feet are now unstable; they can't carry your weight. You cover the toilet bowl and sit on top of it.29

You can't connect the dots looking forward; you can only connect them looking backwards. So you have to trust that the dots will somehow connect in your future. You have to trust in something–your gut, destiny, life, karma, whatever. This approach has never let me down, and it has made all the difference in my life.

Steve Jobs (Co-founder of Apple Computers)

#2: Tears and regrets

*You can't have everything you want,
but you can have the things that really
matter to you. –Marissa Mayer*

You open the letter crying, your tears washing your face. It is unbelievable that after 16 years of dedicated service you are being sent home. The hardwork you had put in building the organization at the expense of your family and happiness is being thrown down the valley.

All the accolades, employee of the year awards are now meaningless, you debate with yourself. How come the other members of staff who are usually late for work and have disciplinary issues are safe and only you is being sent home? Has the Almighty forgotten you? You never miss church, you pay your tithe in equal measure and give offerings, *'why me?'* You ask.

Occurrences in life look so unreal yet real. There is a big difference between movies and reality. To the individual in the mix telling the difference between your reality and the actual reality is extremely a daunting task and impossibility.

What will happen to my family? They are used to having three meals a day, they never lack. How will I pay my bills - the house rent, water, and electricity? What about school fees for my children? There is a car loan monthly deduction. If I don't pay the bank, the asset owners will repossess it. What will my friends in the gated community say, my church faithful, and my friends and not to mention my relatives who asked for my help and I could not assist them –I was truly going through a difficult time.

It has been two hours in the washroom. You cried silently until you slept. You forgot yourself. The sleep brought peace that you have never imagined, not to mention the washroom. It is time to face reality. There is no job for you here. Now you start understanding why news is full of companies retrenching. You ask yourself, why you thought it was okay for others and not you. You pick your letter from the floor, take your handkerchief and dry your face. You start listening if there is any movement in the washroom; you confirm you are all alone.

You wash your face; try to smile at yourself only to see your swollen eyes. You convince yourself life has to go on. You quickly dry your face, hands and go back to the board room; it is the only safe place today. You ask for time to use the laptop promising to leave it at the reception and request to come back after a week for handover.

Reality check

Life has to go on! Crying will not change my current situation. How many people out there survive without employment and lead an honest life? The God I serve will not let me down. Having made the decision to face the future, you leave the company premises. Any other time I visit here I will be as a visitor. You will get used to leaving your national identification card at the gate, waiting for hours on end at the reception to be attended to. People go through hell in this life. Truly they said the wearer of the shoe knows where it pinches most. A story is told of a retired head of state that was used to having the road to himself while travelling. All vehicles on the road were blocked for the VIP (Very Important

Person). On retirement, he became an ordinary VIP; the security personnel were scaled down; people no longer lined the roads to salute him. Other road users cared less when he was passing. Sometimes and in most cases the pecks are for the position and not you!

Another senior executive in a government parastatal was used to having a private lift in a public building. He would not share a lift with ordinary mortals. When his appointment was revoked, life became very difficult. His security fears became magnified. He was seeing fear everywhere. His movements were curtailed by his own fears. I wonder if he feared himself!

Then you remember those investment opportunities that you forewent, you thought saving in a Sacco was for the lowly paid staff. Actually, from your large salary, you could only save KES 1000 per month; it was only after some prodding that you increased your contribution to KES 2000 to keep off critics interfering with your life.

There is a Sacco in Nairobi with an individual who has over 80 million KES in savings. This money generates 10% interest as dividends. The co-operator can comfortably retire on an annual income of 8 million per year. This translates to about KES 666,000 per month. Sacco's are truly for the lowly paid. Since dealing with guarantors is not easy; why not use your pools of accumulation to guarantee yourself?

Then there were the plots being bought along Kangundo road. Who wants to live in Eastlands with the traffic on Jogoo road, Outering and Mombasa road? Kitengela land buying opportunities - no! People lose money buying land with fake titles.

When one is not motivated to do something, there are enough reasons for not doing it. The reasons though may appear rational and well thought out, in reality they are just mere excuses. The individual knows the truth, the solid truth.

I am always doing that which I cannot do, in order that I may learn how to do it.

Pablo Picasso (Spanish painter, poet and playwright)

#3: Strategies on Re-Building Self

The question isn't who is going to let me; it's who is going to stop me. —Ayn Rand

Self - Audit – Face the truth

Find out the real truth about your situation. Have a candid discussion with yourself to understand the real gravity of the current situation. Take a piece of paper and a pen, list all your liabilities (debts) and expenses. Then draw a priority list; taking a keen focus on how you are going to feed yourself and your family. Keep a close eye on huge liabilities that have the capacity to ground you. Auctioneers are not the best company when you are in distress.

Before engaging in anything taxing, have a sincere discussion with your wife or husband (if you are married). It is difficult to break this news to your loved ones. Don't assume life will continue like before. You need income to sort out family expenses and bills. Lay it bare and jointly develop a come-back strategy.

Are there unnecessary assets that you can sell to generate some living expenses? Are you able to move from a three bed - roomed house to one bed - roomed or better still move from up market location to a more affordable residence?

Before the banks start looking for you, are you able to renegotiate the payment terms owing to your current situation? Are you able to get a buyer for your car and get a reasonable offer to help you off-set the car loan balance and get some seed capital to start trading? Alternatively, since you know how to drive can you enrol as an Uber Taxi operator generating daily cash-flow? Accepting the true position and appraising the truth is the beginning of action towards recovery. Remember most successful people have been auctioned severally in their journey to success. Your temporary challenge is a wake-up call for you to dream big, start small and start now!

Get back your economic engine

Take a good look at your skills and abilities. What are you passionate about? Can you play a guitar? Are you able to teach interested parties how to play a guitar at a fee? Do you have accounting skills? There are many entrepreneurs struggling with keeping books of accounts- records and compliance with regulations. Can you become an independent contractor – working at your own pace, time and place?

Scanning the environment, what problem do you think you can solve that people are willing to pay you for taking away the problem? What do you find irritating? It may be your business opportunity. Find out if others are also suffering the same irritant.

The human basic needs for a long time have remained to be food, clothing and housing. Can you supply cooked meals during lunch hour that are affordable, made with love and served with a smile? People are always looking for unique outfits; can you be the designer of choice? Can you help people find houses especially those on transfer using your mobile? You can become a broker. Are you an expert in helping people their problems at a fee?

Can you access a piece of land near a river and become a food producer? There is a growing crave for natural products! Organic foods those are healthy and naturally grown. Can you be the supplier of choice for organic vegetables? Can you collect orders in your gated community for fresh fruits and vegetables and supply the same - you have a car you need to make use of!

Pools of accumulation

With a simple formula one can move from no resources to having some resources. This does not happen by accident. One has to make a conscious decision that they purpose to change their life for the better. The purpose approach is an adequate motivator to drive behaviour change. Remember our thoughts eventually become manifested. Thoughts become actions, actions become habits and habits become character that describes who we are. This is the profound reason why we are warned to mind our thoughts every day.

Now we have a means of earning either by trading or offering some professional service while at the same time solving problems. Even selling vegetables, washing and ironing professionally is a service that can earn one some money. The truth is you don't have to be the one doing it. You can be a go-between.

Cleaning is currently a big industry even in Kenya. Ever wondered how *Parapet*, a cleaning services organization became a major player in office and workspaces cleaning? Cleaning innovatively is a new way of serving clients. Parapet became a disruptor in office cleaning. It provided well trained staff, cleaning tools and flexible cleaning hours outside the normal working hours many were used to. They clean when offices are closed making it ready for you when needed, saving time and money. This empowers the client to concentrate on their core business.

With your new engine of economic empowerment, you are now able to attract some money in your direction in exchange for the service you offer. Is it possible to allocate the revenue in terms of retained profits, a portion ploughed back into the business, a small portion allocated to building a pool of accumulation? This pool of accumulation is a pool of savings that can be used for larger investments in the future.

It is the security for your business, should it encounter problems for example with county government *Askari's,* theft or any other unexpected occurrences.

The pools of accumulation can be saved in a Sacco, *Chama,* table banking and merry go round, where short term lending is acceptable at favourable terms. Building a strong savings culture is a creation of habit. If you can save 20 shillings, 50 shillings, 200 shillings everyday continuously you will have mastered handling money and passed the first step to financial freedom. You cannot invest before you save. Therefore start by saving – building own resources then investing to grow your wealth. You cannot start a business on debt - it will create more problems for you should the business not do well.

Invest in personal development

Many people get into employment and stop investing in personal development. The training courses most employers offer are meant to make you more efficient in building and growing their business. One needs to invest in building their personal brand. There is a difference between the position you occupy and you. Failure to recognize this is the reason many people feel stressed, annoyed and bitter when they are replaced or sacked.

Building your personal brand is making you more marketable, equipping self with an array of skills and abilities you can tap on. How do you build your personal brand? To build your brand, one needs to select skills to develop especially the soft skills; people skills. Attending seminars, reading books and taking a deliberate decision to better yourself and better your life.

Invest in Relationships

Many known, international and local inspiration speakers argue that; it is the people you meet and the books you read that will change your life. I hasten to add that this primarily is based on a premise that people are the ultimate source of progress. The books you read are almost the same as meeting the authors since you can read their thoughts and mind-set.

Investing in healthy relationships can help you grow in interpersonal relationships; knowing how to handle people. This also helps one in becoming a better communicator and knowing how to develop through learning from others.

Jim Rohn asserts that you are the average of the 5 people in your circle of influence. If everyone in your circle of influence is always complaining, it means you also complain a lot. The vibes among your association resonate without resistance, since all members of the group are comfortable with each other. Dear reader, I advise changing your association to people who will challenge you, make you uncomfortable and develop you. In the discomfort compete with your potential; not members of the group. All roads lead to Rome, your success route may be different but the process is the same.

Invest in continuous learning

Investing in continuous learning makes one better every time. For one to succeed in whatever field one chooses, one needs to aspire being the best in that field. It is through being the best in your trade, skills and experiences that one attracts top dollars.

Challenge your thoughts, listen to positive vibes DVD's, CD's and educative materials. Practice what you learn and think; it is beneficial. It is through creating a habit that we become better.

Looking around the world; the best comedians, musicians, athletes and stock traders are those at the top 1%. They attract fees or income many times the average in the industry. Simply put, be the best. Why is it that the CEO of an organization earns 4-10 million per month and in the same organization there is an employee earning 20,000 shillings per month in wages?

Success principles are universal. The same "lowly" paid staff can turn his/her 20,000 shillings income into a multi - million shillings investment with the right strategies solving a problem in the world. How big is the problem you want to solve? How fast and how efficiently are you going to do it? Get a mentor to walk with you, learning is priceless. There is no luxury of time to make mistakes that one can avoid through mentorship.

Model your role model. It is called visualization - see yourself doing better than your role model. Explore the world, read about the person you admire and would like to acquire some of their skills and the habits. Read anything published in print and social media about your model. Pick the skills and habits that will make you a better person.

Believe in yourself

You have immense potential in you. If you are able to put your mind, soul, heart and gut, in what you have chosen to pursue, you will be unstoppable. The challenges that look insurmountable are just your imaginations, your thoughts. The logic is simple; how do you eat an elephant? Simply one bite after another. This needs to be your mantra to succeed in any difficult task. As Mubarak Munyika, a youthful self-taught computer geek, says "If you find yourself competing against intelligent Africans, with a plan and strategy you need to be intelligent, have a plan and strategy in addition, you need speed and aggressiveness to achieve anything significant"

I conclude by quoting a great son of Africa Mr. Kene Mpkaru, the founder of Film House Cinema brand, who decided when he was 14 years old that he *"would learn what it takes, understand what is required and implement what is needed"* This is a powerful mantra we need to adopt if we purpose to achieve anything valuable in life.

Man cannot discover new oceans unless he has the courage to lose sight of the shore.

–Andre Paul Guillaume Gide (French Author and Nobel Laurent)

#4: From Zero to Significance

The most important thing to remember is this: to be ready at any moment to give up what you are for what you might become. -W. E. B. Du Bois

Sometimes in life you have to lose what you have to be catapulted to your full potential. The motivation to go after something better comes during times of hardship. We need to relook our moments of hardship with the perspective of understanding the lessons hidden within them.

Joan was born in Eldoret in the 1970's. She schooled in Nakuru (Standard One), before continuing her primary school studies in Nyeri. She was forced to repeat Standard Two in Nyeri Primary School where she finished as the Pioneer Class of Standard 8 in the year 1985. She attended secondary school in Mukurwe-ini, South Tetu Girls High School, where she excelled in creative design activities contributing to the school logo, at concept development stage. She passed her Form Four in the year 1989 and proceeded to Kenya Polytechnic to study Legal Secretarial. Her fees was paid save for the last year of study.

College fees became a challenge since she had lost her dad in October, 1992. A visit to the Dean of Students by chance got her a scholarship for the last term through Rantasi Trust Fund! Upon graduation she was employed in a law firm, in the year 1995 as a receptionist. Within a short time due to her expertise, she was promoted to a secretary. She worked for this particular law firm for 7 years. The partnership encountered a problem and was dissolved leaving Joan jobless.

After a brief sabbatical of 5-8 months, Joan got another placement in a law firm where she worked as a senior secretary and personal assistant to the managing partner to the law firm. Here she worked for another 7 years. On the side she ran a fashion boutique. She would leave Kenya on Friday night for Dubai, South Africa, Thailand or Uganda and shop on Saturday have the goods shipped to Kenya and fly back on Sunday ready for work on Monday.

She started this business with just 100,000 shillings and grew it to about 500,000. The biggest cost was tickets; it was lucrative then and not as crowded as it is today. This business collapsed when she loaned a relative KES 250,000/- which she has not recovered to date. Some of her stock she had sold on credit could not be recovered. A preview of why businesses fail.

Shortly after her business collapsed she was laid off in the year 2009. She was then expecting her second born. She was not happy where she worked due to the restrictive nature of the work environment. There was idleness, once her routine work was done. She cried on her way home not knowing how she was going to survive.

At the bus station she sat on a bench pondering what next. She had no energy to get home. Ruaka residence distance from town appeared to have doubled on this day. She had a 3 year old child born in 2007 and was expecting another. How could life be so cruel?

She became a house wife for a while, as she nursed her second born in 2010. It was a difficult period of her life. She would contact her law clerks friends who would offer her some work making about 200- 500 per day. This delegation is called being a minion. Law clerks with a lot of work would contract friends to assist them finish their errands on time.

After her son was born, a sister - in -law assisted her to get employment in another law firm which wanted a secretary. Joan wanted a conveyancing job that allowed her some freedom out of the office. The office environment was a bit restrictive. The advocate accepted and a new life started for Joan. Having experienced job losses before, she needed to be in a position to generate some extra income as she worked. In the one year she worked she used to get her own clients who needed help with processing land documents at *Ardhi* house.

There was a client who wanted some job done and having been frustrated for quite some time with the encumbrances placed on his way, Joan managed to process and deliver work earning her a handsome commission. This client became useful when Joan was out of employment. He referred a good number of clients to her.

A relative wished to sell her properties in Nairobi and relocate to Nakuru. Joan was tasked with selling most of the properties. She managed to interest a client who went viewing one of the properties, then engaged a former employer to undertake due diligence. The land was being sold for KES 20 million. This was a good commission compared to the peanuts she used to earn in employment. The mighty salary can be blinding! She was again challenged by her Aunt to sell a 120 acre farm. She managed to get a client and closed the deal. This opened her eyes to the potential in the real estate sector. God was faithful to Joan. She could sell properties, manage properties, organize land valuation and offer conveyancing consulting services. The series of sales continued and Joan decided to organize her business by getting an office, increasing her service offering and being serious with her work. She managed to purchase her first car from conveyancing commissions.

In 2013 she opened her office, furnished it with furniture from the house. She spruced up the furniture to exhibit a new image-brand building. The colour coding and matching as part of branding was also settled on. She enrolled at Strathmore Business School in the year 2013 under the SEDC programme to understand finances, taxation, marketing, human resource management and general business operations.

The trainings at Strathmore University gave Joan business structure and vision. She appreciated the role of employees in a business.

In the property market there were many players who also happen to be sound business partners, therefore, she needed to understand the roles clearly and gain clarity of the vision for her business. She started by opening an office in Ngara in 2013 and worked for three years before relocating in July, 2016 to her current office address in Ruaka. Joan had a pillar in her late dad, Mr. Joseph Karuiru Miano. She learnt business operations under his mentorship. Her father was a graduate of Egerton University College in Njoro, Nakuru. He worked with Kenya Cooperative Creameries before resigning and venturing into business. He was among the pioneers of selling Chicken and Chips in Nakuru under the brand Rift Rosters. He also invested in a construction company. He was an ambitious man who tried his luck on elective positions unsuccessfully.

The businesses collapsed once he joined politics! Joan's father was jailed in the year 1986 and was released from prison in 1989. Once released, he decided to start a tomato sauce manufacturing venture from the house, where young Joan used to be the Operations Manager. Here she earned her first salary of six hundred shillings (KES 600/=). She helped in the design and concept of the labels. The business grew until it was moved to a manufacturing site in a Godown in Free Area, Nakuru. The proprietor invited Kenya Bureau of Standards (KEBS) for inspection and offering a standardization mark. The business was doing well until Joan went back to college, at the same time the father started ailing. The business eventually collapsed after all the investment.

The people you align yourself with and model have an impact on the way you think. Joan has been attending various seminars by Dr. Miles Monroe, Dr. Cindy Trimm, James Karundu and Bishop Allan Kyuna where she learnt about investing in oneself; believe in one's ability and trusting in God by putting Him before anything!

In her vision in the property business, there are seven arms that all impact positively to humanity, creating a difference. The pillars are Miamu Properties, Handy cleaning services, Training and events, Movers, Financial services, Sacco and lastly a mobile App. The pillars are actively being developed into the business.

Joan is going places. She has been invited to the USA & UK to develop how she can offer services to the Diaspora. Many people have lost money using relatives as points of contact in their investments. Here one needs to read 'The Richest Man in Babylon' by George Clason, who advices "you cannot trust a carpenter with insights of investing in Gold or a blacksmith with taking care of flock".

Lessons learnt

You cannot work alone - First and foremost God needs to be a stakeholder in one's business. Secondly, you need people to succeed. People create useful associations and networks that every business needs.

The other fundamental lesson she learnt is that business is not as hard as people take it to be. It is doable with the right mind-set, will and discipline.

Business is steered by sales, selling products or services. This is what will make a business successful - your happy customers, served by your valued employees.

Challenges in a business are normal, especially managing cash-flow throughout the year is necessary for survival and growth.

Advice to others

Just start. The idea you are joking with is with many people. If you don't start you will see someone who is brave enough has already implemented your idea. "There is nothing new under the sun".

Work with goals and monitor your progress, celebrate the milestones and improve as you go.

Work for God, your legacy and serve to succeed.

When you play it too safe, you're taking the biggest risk of your life. Time is the only wealth we're given.

Barbara Sher (Speaker, Life Coach and Author)

#5: From Ashes to Success

Life is inherently risky. There is only one big risk you should avoid at all costs, and that is the risk of doing nothing. –Denis Whitley

Sarah Karingi is a go - getter. She is determined to pursue her dreams whatever the situation. She started her schooling in Kirinyaga for lower primary and completed her primary schooling in Embu. It's in Embu that she also completed secondary school as well as her "A" levels. She then pursued a Bachelor of Commerce degree specializing in Marketing at The University of Nairobi.

Her early employment was as a civil servant having worked with the Ministry of Finance and Kenya Revenue Authority (KRA) before venturing into business. She has expertise in business management as well as taxation. The entrepreneurship bug gets its captives in life sometimes early; sometimes late. While working as a civil servant, she spotted opportunities to make extra money for herself. Occasionally, she would procure high quality used clothes from Gikomba open air market; wash, iron and then package them nicely. With this value addition she could charge premium prices. It is easy to transform 500 shillings into 2000 shillings by just value addition. Her clothing business was popular with colleagues at work who had no time to shop and wanted to look good, fashionable and trendy.

When mobile telephony was introduced in Kenya in 1999, it was another opportunity to make money. Since sourcing mobiles was not as easy then, as it is today, people who had travelled before could source mobiles in bulk for wholesale resale to potential retailers. Early bird - first mover advantage gives one an opportunity to make tidy profits. With the income supplementation, she managed to help contribute in building the family business.

As a civil servant she worked in finance, this exposure helped her acquire experience that she used in record keeping for the family business. Here she worked over the weekends or when on vacation learning about the business. Her spouse was an Architect who believed in self-employment. Apart from designing projects he would help clients with fittings from his wood products manufacturing factory.

The timber business was purchased in 1996. Initially, the new owners made business mistakes like buying timber with defects and not knowing where to source good timber at good prices. Learning in entrepreneurship is occasionally an experiential learning pursuit. Slowly they mastered the art of sourcing outside the country with reliable suppliers and achieving better trade margins.

Lack of hands on presence in the business requires use of business systems that work to your advantage. Being able to prevent pilferage by employees and keeping proper records not only for tax purposes but being able to appreciate the health of your enterprise. Running several businesses calls for proper business systems. As an entrepreneur, have a way of interacting with sources of information and building your ability to learn. Your customers, suppliers and employees are rich sources of information and knowledge sometimes disruptive. In the family business, the core values of integrity, team work, efficiency and professionalism are practiced. All customer inquiries and quotations are dealt with speed. The business has incorporated the use of technology to help with systems and security.

Early in life Sarah and her family decided to take life insurance. Little did they know it would one day be a source of funds: it reduced serious financial exposure much later in life. Don't mind the waiting and the insurance company's reluctance to honour their obligations, eventually they pay.

Sarah worked for almost 18 years before leaving the civil service in 2003. Her superiors were fond of her dedication and hard work. She jokes that her resignation letter was kept for three months just in case she changed her mind she would still get her job back. At any opportunity to serve, we need to build healthy relationships geared towards propelling the organizations into efficiency and productivity. This focus does not only serve the organization but also builds a habit and character that one needs later for other opportunities.

Businesses have challenges that many people will never appreciate. With a business, as the owner, you have responsibility over other families apart from your own. Other people's livelihood depends on you.

In 2003, Sarah's spouse got unwell. This forced Sarah to stop working and help in the family business as she also took care of her family. The timber factory dealt with selling raw timber as well as processed timber. They sold fittings, doors, frames and most timber products. She had to learn the business fast, make decisions regarding the business - called being thrown in the deep sea to swim with the sharks. Many of her friends discouraged her and some of the workers doubted her potential.

It takes time to build confidence in workers. The business was servicing a bank loan. The family had some rental units where they were getting some passive income. The rental units were being managed through an agent. Due to absence of the founder, the business started suffering. Some tenants also stopped paying for their occupancy.

Shortly in 2006, Sarah's husband rested. Many people discouraged Sarah on her managing the family business. They didn't know her resolve and determination to succeed was fixed and non-negotiable.

A number of employees left and some remained - those who were determined to see her succeed. Those who left were actually workers who had other motivations. Sarah was now on the driver's seat, making sure that customers were served and their needs taken care of. Sarah believed in The Almighty, she had self-belief and had invested in learning and consulting friends in the industry- other architects. She transitioned fast into routine management of the business learning experientially.

One Sunday in the year 2010 at around 1.30pm, the guard left shortly to take lunch and then the unthinkable happened. The factory was razed by fire to the ground. Nothing could be salvaged. The timing was 'perfect'. There was no work going on in the workshop, all machines were off. There was no possible source of fire apart from arson.

The culprit must have been a person with inside information. This experience was a tough one. The business was serving a bank loan, workers needed to be paid, there was no other reliable source of income and children were in school. The main source of income was razed to the ground.

At 4.30pm, Sarah finally managed to get to the business premises since she had travelled out of town. There was a drive to give-up, neighbours expected her to faint which she didn't. The damage was massive, stocks gone, machines damaged - it was a colossal damage. Relatives kept off, friends kept off- sometimes in the thicket of things your true friends are easy to spot; they are not many. She remembers some neighbours giving her 12,000 to console her after a few days. Customers disappeared. Suppliers also disappeared.

Rebuilding the business

Sarah was left with one supplier who believed in her. She visited the bank to try re-negotiating the loan- she was not successful. She was advised to make payments without delay. When in real problems it is good to share what you are going through - help may just get to you. The employees stood by her. She collected money from other projects that were running or completed to get some start-up capital for operations. She started by getting spares - repairing damaged machines, one after another. One spares suppliers stood by her through all the difficult times and is still a good supplier to date.

Sarah joined Business Networks International (BNI), having learned the power of networking and its effect on business growth. That decision was a game changer. One would get connections to new customers as you build your business. She learned marketing, management, building teams and ICT- computer knowledge. Sarah became digital.

She then embarked on roofing the sites where the machines were as she continued operations. Roofing the whole factory took more than a year. She finished roofing in 2016. That year, previous customers started streaming back. Partnerships built on trust;

integrity and honesty overcome most challenges. Relationships with workers, suppliers and customers need to be protected in honesty. She sold other assets, pieces of land to finance the timber business.

To run a business successfully, one has to invest in personal development. Sarah underwent entrepreneurship training under Strathmore Business School programme (SEDC). She networks and always believes in giving referrals to other entrepreneurs. She has grown both in business and personally. She managed to take her children through college successfully. She has increased products that her business offers to include building materials supplies like sand, ballast and building stones.

She motivates her employees, many who have worked with the establishment for over 15 years. The employees are actually partners in the business. They give suggestions on the ways to improve the business.

Many times their suggestions have led to innovations in the business and revenue generation. The employees have knowledge of the business and know the customers well. They appreciate having worked with Sarah. Their families have grown, some got married, build homes in their rural areas and now they are working towards acquiring plots in Nairobi.

With frequent power black-outs in Nairobi, employees once suggested to Sarah to invest in a big generator that could run her business operations. This, indeed, was an opportunity. When many places have no power, your customers actually increase. Thinking innovatively can render competition irrelevant. Build additional revenues and customer bases.

Learning how to use technology to improve operations in her business was a very good insight. Today there is no need to move from one area to another trying to compare prices of supplies. A call, email, WhatsApp communication is indeed cheaper and faster. Her determination enabled her to overcome all challenges and come out victorious.

Your attitude is a key mind-set programmer for success. Believing moving forward irrespective of challenges. You can ask for advice, consult but NEVER GIVE UP. Follow your gut. In situations of discouragement and hopelessness, follow your gut feeling. The solution to moving forward is trapped deep inside you. Sarah is a director to several companies where her leadership and networks are valued.

Lessons from Sarah

- When in problems, focus on solving the problem one step at a time. Crying about the past doesn't help; focus on the present and where you want to go. Focus on the priority areas with the resources you have at that moment.

- People are always willing to help - talk about what you need; you never know who is listening, ready and willing to help. Referrals are strong channels of building a viable business. Let people know what you do and what you need.

- Talk to creditors - even when you have no money to pay. Whenever you get some income, pay down your debt. Building a credit history of consistency gives you an edge in the market.

- Investing in reliable and dependable employees is a pillar to building a viable, sustainable and efficient business. When your employees believe they can trust you as an employer; they will give their all to ensure your business succeeds whatever the challenge.

- Networking is a business game-changer. It fortifies your customers. It is effective and profitable if you maintain legitimacy, honesty and deliver consistently. Listen to your customers always.

#6: From Loss to Better Focus

If you are not willing to risk the unusual, you will have to settle for the ordinary. –Jim Rohn

Life has many phases. It is never a straight line. We are surprised when we do all the right things but what comes out of our direction is never palatable. One can be a faithfully practicing Christian, paying tithe, giving offerings, remembering our Creator in prayer, fasting and thanksgiving. Then why does misfortune follow us?

Calisto Omondi was born in Ugenya, Siaya County and spent his earlier life in Ugenya before moving to Nairobi. His father was working as a Store Clerk for a public secondary school in Nairobi. He went to school in his rural village then attended secondary school in Kisii. He attended "A" levels in Nairobi then joined Egerton University in Njoro, eventually graduating from with a Degree in Economics and Statistics. He was employed by the government as an Assistant Economist in 1991. He worked as a Civil Servant for three years. This was a wonderful opportunity. There was so much time available in between projects. It is a good working environment if one is considering studying; the pay though was not much.

As life would have it, financial demands increase when one starts their own family. Calisto opted for greener pastures offering better remuneration in terms of salary, medical cover and better career progression opportunities. Marriage changes things. He left public service and joined an international private university in Nairobi as an administrator. Here he worked for 5 years. To enhance his career prospects, Calisto enrolled for a post graduate diploma in Computer Science at The University of Nairobi, graduating two years later in the year 2002. With the newly acquired technical skills, he tried transiting from administration routine work to Information Technology within his then employer, the private university to no avail as he was informed that there were no suitable vacancies.

Networking is a powerful tool in career progression and business growth. With the help of contacts of former students at the university where he worked, he joined an international software company as a Junior Consultant in 2002, having applied, got interviewed and was placed after 4 months.

The salary and total package was much better than at the previous employer. He was now a practicing IT Consultant. For two years things ran smoothly and it was a wonderful work environment. Working among young people, self-driven, agile and trying new things was quite a relief from routine administrative work.

In business, there are factors outside the work environment that can affect business operations. There was a change in regime in Kenya. This meant that the way business was done in the past changed. Sourcing new business became a challenge for the software company. With scarcity of new projects and with current projects all coming to an end with no new ones, the company turned all consultants into sales staff and the transition was not smooth for the affected staff. This went on for about five months with little success. In the meantime, the consultants now turned sales team, were able to collect data on computer systems used by Large and Small and Middle -sized Enterprises (SMEs) with the aim of finding innovative ways to serve them. The only challenge was the revenue generated was not sustainable to keep the company running. After five months, hard decisions had to be made and the CEO from Spain cracked the whip with a downsizing strategy.

The various project managers were tasked with trimming the work force. One morning, Calisto was asked to a meeting and his project manager delivered the bad news and gave him the letter relieving him of his duties. She apologized saying "Nothing personal. Should things change, we will call you. You are a valued team member". Calisto was in the process of receiving a loan he had applied for earlier from his Sacco for a project at his rural home. He had to stop the loan process following his retrenchment.

With a retrenchment letter on his hand, confused and thinking about his family, it was quite a depressing phase in his life. Where do you take your family living in a rented house? After a sober discussion with self, the spouse and after looking at all situations critically, he decided life had to go on. Our friend Calisto resolved not to keep the problem with him since a problem shared is half solved. He shared with friends and his social networks. It was not long before a friend who was a Dean at a private university called him for an interview for a teaching position in that university. This he did for one semester. Within this time, a job offer for an IT Manager was advertised within the Conference of Bishops of one of the mainstream Churches in Kenya. Calisto applied for this job and got it. He worked there for almost two years.

First things first, while working at the Bishop's Conference, the family bought a plot in Syokimau, in the outskirts of Nairobi, along Mombasa Road on the eastern side of Jomo Kenyatta International Airport. Thank God it was not in the area that had demolitions - this would have been catastrophic.

Now working at the conference of bishops, things seemed fine. But it was not long before things changed rapidly. The Conference of Bishops was dependent on donor funds for various projects. With a change in regime, it took about two years before the donor community started embracing the new government. The bulk of donor money that was initially going to the Church and Church based organizations was now being channelled through the government as budget support for its numerous programmes like free primary education, judicial reforms among others. Organizations with integrity issues suffered the most. With the dried donor funds, it did not take long before the Church decided to keep the core functions and do away with support functions and a second retrenchment occurred! This one came in a very inhumane way. Changes were eminent and December holidays were fast approaching. The leadership took the opportunity of the people being away on vacation to send retrenchment letters via post office. Staff members who received their letters first called others to check their post office mails. No official communication such as a telephone call to the affected staff was ever made by the leadership not withstanding that this is a Church organization with religious leaders who, ideally, should have a more humane demeanour! Nowadays, others are sacked through a phone call, a text message or even worse, an email.

With a second retrenchment letter in his hands, Calisto had to think and act fast if he was to remain sane and this he did. Drastic times call for drastic measures. What next? He visited his plot at Syokimau and inquired from a neighbour who was already settled there on what he needed to do, to stay on his plot. Based on the information he gathered from the neighbour, he knew that the only source of funds available to the family at that time, were the savings from his Sacco. Calisto therefore resigned from his Sacco and collected his savings totalling to approximately KES 120,000. With this money, he went ahead and fenced the plot, dug a pit latrine and acquired a dog for security. He then built a two-roomed tin structure with cemented floor and moved his family. This took away the rent problem. Some of his furniture was left with relatives in the wider Nairobi since the house was too small to accommodate everything he owned. In the meantime, their daughter would complain that her class mates were ridiculing her in school saying they were poor. Calisto encouraged the daughter, who was exemplarily bright, not to mind people she beats in class who are looking for ways of crashing her spirit.

Five months after the second retrenchment, Calisto was getting short term engagements while networking with his friends and his social and professional networks. The big break came when a former college mate was transiting to a new firm and a replacement was urgently required. Calisto was called for an interview and got the job based on his skills and experience. The friend helped him settle in his role fast by offering to train him on the job in the evening for a few days. He still works for this company 11 years down the line and even his spouse currently works for the same organization.

With the support of his wife, Calisto has now built a seven-bedroomed house on his plot. He has invested for posterity and the family is comfortable. The children are attending good schools and the first one having passed her primary and secondary school examinations very well, is currently a sophomore studying for a Bachelor's Degree in Law at a top private university. The other two children are in lower primary and high school respectively, also in good private schools. The family has two cars and the first-born daughter has a car at her disposal to commute to college daily. The family is happy and still together. Love in the family has been nurtured. The foundation becomes stronger when challenges occur but what makes the difference is how you tackle the challenges. You may take the challenges head on or succumb. In life, things like retrenchment are triggers that help us to change the course of our life for the better and without them; our eyes may never be opened even to glaring opportunities ahead. Moreover, God allows them to happen. While this is a story with a happy ending, I am aware that not all retrenchments or even double retrenchments like this end up this way. Some end up in family break-ups, suicides and other extremes. What makes the difference?

The difference rests with the support structure one has developed over time combined with total submission to God's will. In this case, we can see that Calisto had a good network of real friends and a very supportive spouse. The family members are spiritual lot. The two children were still too young to be a source of real stress. All these factors and other silent ones, made the difference.

Whichever way you look at it, retrenchment leaves families with very limited options. Extended family may help one with food occasionally but it is highly unlikely that they pay rent for the affected kin hence securing shelter early enough in one's working life is critical.

While retrenchment for any individual; whether man or woman is very devastating, men seem to be more vulnerable of the two genders. Mr. Calisto feels for men who get suddenly retrenched. It is a humbling as well as a humiliating experience for a man to lose a job in this manner. A man feels lost, empty and insufficient when faced with a sudden loss of a job and some never recover from it. This is because most men are defined by their jobs and careers, unfortunate as it is. But like from his experience, it is not the end of the world! There is life after retrenchment and this is what this chapter is all about. God never gives you more than you can handle. 1 Cor. 10: 13 (No trial has come to you but what is human. God is faithful and will not let you be tried beyond your strength, but with the trial, he will also provide a way out, so that you may be able to bear it).

God never forsakes His flock if they remain spiritually grounded and look up upon Him.

Lessons from Calisto

- When in problems network with close friends, don't hide.
  Truth and integrity will sort you out.
- Invest in continuous learning; learn new skills, and build Excellence.
- Invest in a piece of land - it may be your new home.

I have no special gift. I am only passionately curious

Albert Einstein (German physicist)

#7: From Pain to Wealth

Only those who will risk going too far can possibly find out how far one can go. –T. S. Eliot

Mercy is a visionary, able to see opportunities and grow businesses out of the identified opportunities. She is a dynamite; unstoppable. She is a start-up specialist. She is able to identify an investment opportunity, gather resources and create a business. She doesn't procrastinate, she acts with finality. Her life journey reads like a fairy tale. She started her early schooling in Muranga, secondary school in Kiambu later joining The University of Nairobi for a diploma in Early Childhood Development and sign language specialization. She later graduated with a Bachelor's Degree. Mercy is gifted in marketing, training and people development.

She started learning business early in life. Her parents were professionals; the father a medical doctor in private practice running a hospital and her mother a teacher. They would help in the family businesses. She desired to learn and also be a professional. Her first job was at a local public university where she worked as an administrator and sign language interpreter. She wanted to become a university don.

The more things change the more we are forced to modify our plans. She started with a temporary agreement, later changed to yearly renewable contracts with a promise to permanent engagement in the future, with no pressure on the employer. As an employee, this is a wonderful arrangement an employer who does not want to commit is actually telling you, "Gain experience, learn and build networks at my expense."

After a few years of service, Mercy went on leave and that is when issues started stalking her. One never knows what plans other colleagues have in their minds. Usually Mercy helped with drawing proposals for funding to support students with disability in the institution and it was up to the head of department to account for all expenditure after training workshops.

When Mercy was away there were reports that there were issues in her absence and this raised accountability issues necessitating her contract to be put on hold. On her return, her salary had not been paid. On further inquiry at the bank, she was advised to check with her employer since other colleagues had already been paid.

On reporting being friendly as usual she realized something was wrong. A fellow member of staff commented "you have been lost" another said, "we tried looking for you and you couldn't be found" these were tell-tale signs things were not okay.

On inquiring about her salary, the bombshell dropped; she had a case to answer! How and where, she was never involved in accounting. It was not among her deliverables. She was informed that there were funds which were not adequately accounted for. As the issue was investigated, Mercy had no salary, no other source of income and had to report on duty as usual. The matter reached the university senate. Mercy was indeed found innocent. She had stayed for four months without a salary.

Operating in Nairobi without income is not an easy matter. Mercy faced reality, she had to survive, go to work every day and 91 **From Pain to Wealth** pay for all bills. A way had to be found or innovated. Mercy's mother would send food to her. Her only problem now was how to commute to work and how to pay rent. Being a trained teacher, she started offering tuition classes for neighbours at 500 shillings per child per month.

Earlier, she had assisted her sister join a Network Marketing (NWM) firm. Network marketing is the new way of doing business. It is quite successful in the USA. In her mind, this was just to keep her sister busy since it was not a "proper" business. She didn't see it as an opportunity. That was in 2003. One day, her sister had used the 200 shillings that was meant for their transport back home. With only 40 shillings they could not get means back home and it was also late they couldn't walk home for security reasons. It was a bad day, being broke. They were forced to keep busy in town until the fares went down. They decided to join NWM presentations to pass time.

With time the presentations appeared like a real money making opportunity. The only problem was they had no money to invest to become members. It was then that the sister informed Mercy that she was indeed a member, and what was needed were products to sell. It was at this opportune time that they remembered they had products in the house that they could use as starter packs.

Excited with the new opportunity, they went home. It was refreshing to see in the meeting people clapping, receiving cheques on their achievements. It was a money making opportunity. Mercy and the sister joined hands to exploit this opportunity. With the price list, training and mentorship, her journey of working part-time selling multi-level products began.

The next day at 6am in the morning she was required in town to be trained by a new mentor in sales. Leaving the house very early was advantageous since fares were even cheaper. By 5.30 am, Mercy was in town waiting for the trainer. At exactly 6.00am, at Hornbill (a restaurant in town), the trainer/mentor arrived. They prepared a list of people to target and worked on generating 300 shillings income per day for the next one month. Mercy repackaged washing powder product in sachets that could be retailed at 100 shillings each. Her goal was to sell to three people daily at the least. This is a lesson in goal setting.

By the second month Mercy was generating sales of 500 shillings daily. With this she saved 200 shillings and used the 300 for her expenses. In one year she had saved about 62,600 shillings. With NWM, she learned how to sell, time management, goal setting and being your own boss. She believed her mentor, "if one can sell a product for 30 shillings he/she can sell products for 1000 shillings". Mercy set out to work.

The sales experience getting another stream of income was a real eye opener. One realizes that time is a resource that needs to be used judiciously. She organized product demonstration early in the morning, lunch time and after work. Saturdays were occupied - she was recruiting clients through demonstration. Mercy was the most efficient employee at her place of work. She would be the earliest in office daily. She worked tirelessly to serve her work clients, clearing her work quota with renewed motivation.

In only 4 months, Mercy was able to match her day jobs salary with that from the multi-level marketing job. This meant she had two salaries for the same period. Other opportunities opened up. Mercy recommends one to surround oneself with pillars of support when in difficulty. Be among positive people to help renew your energy. There is no impossibility - everything you put your mind in is possible. She invested in personal development through trainings and books. She recommends a book *"Let Go of Whatever Makes You Stop"* by John Mason. Another excellent book on relationships is Dale Carnegie's *"How to Win Friends and Influence People"*

Mercy was highly motivated and unstoppable. She would buy used clothes in Gikomba, wash, iron and package to add value then sell at a premium. She would sell socks, bedsheets and duvets. She was dependable. She would be given orders in advance in some cases and Mercy would deliver. She couldn't afford to disappoint. Trading helped her achieve her goals. She leads a goal driven life. She was the best worker by 2005 at the University. By 2007, she was earning four times her salary. Mercy is an avid saver. Most of the bonuses she achieved were invested in property. Land is a good asset that grows one's money slowly and surely. Mercy decided to resign to concentrate on her business full time. The boss refused to sign her resignation. Mercy had already decided to leave. You know your value to an organization when your exit is untenable. Busy people are the most organized. Mercy would serve her business clients from 7am-8am then concentrate on her day job till 5pm then embark on her selling hustle. She couldn't believe that multi-level marketing came to her rescue when her salary was wrongly stopped.

Television watching is a waste of time. One is better off reading a book or listening to audios or DVD's for personal development. In 2008, Mercy started freelance sign language interpretation. It was racking in good income, the only problem was the business was not easy to scale since clients get used to only preferring the business owner.

Multi-level marketing succeeds due to social networks which are also referred to as social capital. It is a source of resources as well as a "market". The network is a market that waits for one to exploit. Mercy registered a company to run her consultancy and agency work. She maintained a strong network of rural farmers who were a market for her NWM business. This was her blue ocean, as many people concentrate in towns. Mercy concentrated serving farmers three times a week opened a door to other opportunities in terms of farm produce sales.

She started *Chaqula* business venture specializing in selling fresh fruits and vegetables to her neighbours and other clienteles she developed while giving talks on nutrition and its benefits to corporates. Mercy is a networker and believes in connecting with your customers to be able to grow successfully. The fresh food has grown into a full fledge standalone business delivering fresh fruits, vegetables and fish. Food supplies is a profitable business if you can source properly, affordably, have efficient logistics and consistency.

Anyone can be a business partner in terms of sources of information. Watchmen, human resource staff, and messengers can contribute to your success. Investing in continuous learning is a game changer in business. Having attended Growth Oriented Women Enterprises (GOWE) training opened her eyes on how a business is run professionally. She was able to understand why successful people have many businesses and they are not struggling. Having systems and structures in the business is the name of the game.

Another opportunity for training with an international franchise, Dale Carnegie, opened up. Mercy went to the USA for training and came back a master trainer. She is an expert in soft skills training. She ran the franchise with a partner for two years, exiting in 2015. Mercy advises, one needs to build one business for three years before investing in another opportunity. This strategy will enable one to continuously build successful businesses repeatedly.

Her advice is you can't do it alone. You need to have a structured partnership for one to realize his/her full potential. With partners aligned in business they are able to bake a bigger cake and pitch for bigger jobs where everyone is a winner.

Lessons from Mercy

- Learning how to sell is a useful skill in life.
- Believe in yourself, if you don't, no one will believe in You.
- Opportunities are where you are; look no further.

#8: Not Giving up

The universe has no restrictions. You place restrictions on the universe with your expectations. –Deepak Chopra

Life has an interesting way of rewarding those who persist and quitters alike. To the persistent; the returns are huge and fulfilling, the quitters are full of regrets and bitterness. Friend, you have a choice to chart your own path. Success is no respecter of family background, experience, connections or level of education. Find a big problem in the world, solve it and you will surely be successful.

In this chapter, let's reflect on two great sons of Africa who found themselves in different situations and came out victorious. Quitting is not a solution neither is it an option for you in your journey of success. You have all you need to chart your own course in life. We have unlimited potential, we are the only ones placing limits in what we can do or achieve.

Engineer Strive Masiyiwa

Mr. Strive Masiyiwa is a self-made billionaire; he is estimated to be worth over $600 million in personal wealth (Forbes, 2015). He was born in 1961. He took his early education in Zambia, secondary schooling in Scotland and eventually graduated with an electrical engineering degree from the University of Wales.

Engineer Masiyiwa was employed in 1984, in the telecommunications sector in a Zimbabwean state corporation. He resigned to start his own enterprise with only $75 and today he is a leading investor, industrialist and well known as a philanthropist. He started Econet wireless - his first enterprise. I happened to attend a seminar that the soft spoken Masiyiwa shared his story. One time he went to a bank to ask for credit and he couldn't qualify like many start-ups. The bank manager, a lady asked the young engineer if the sleek car he was driving in then was his. He replied in the affirmative. The bank manager challenged him to sell off the car and the bank would match what he would have collected. As they say the rest is history.

Engineer Masiyiwa was denied a license to operate a private telecommunication company since the government entity then, was a state monopoly. Rather than accept the status quo or complain, Mr. Masiyiwa decided to fight the monopoly status through the court system. The battle almost crippled him financially. It was a long 5 year battle which he won. He started his outfit Econet Wireless in 1998 dealing in mobile telephony having recognized the need to connect majority of the African population.

Econet Wireless has a subscriber base of over 9 million in Zimbabwe; it is listed in the country's stock exchange. This is the most profitable corporate organization in Zimbabwe and the second largest in market capitalization. This entrepreneur expanded to South Africa where he started Econet group independent of the Zimbabwean operations. He expanded to Nigeria, Ghana, Botswana, Rwanda, Burundi, Kenya, UK, UAE, Latin America, New Zealand as well as China.

In 2008, He moved to United Kingdom where he established Liquid Telecom group that led to the intercontinental expansion through fibre optics and satellite. He has invested in financial sectors, insurance, renewable energy and solar solutions. He is a Global Investor.

Botswana story in his own words

The audacity of faith calls for a lot of preparation and practice. Listen to me, child of Africa, (and indeed any entrepreneur from wherever you are): It is doable!

Here's a story, before: When the government of Botswana issued a tender for two mobile licenses in 1997, they hired a team of international experts from Sweden to help adjudicate offers from five companies. There were five bidders: MTN, Vodacom (in partnership with Botswana Telecoms), Bharti of India, France Telecom (Orange) and Mascom Wireless (the name I gave my consortium, which was short for Masiyiwa Communications). The consultants advising the Botswana Telecoms Authority asked each bidder to come make a pitch and answer questions. A full day was set aside for each bidder.Our competitors came in private jets. On our side, some members of my team travelled by car from Harare in Zimbabwe (a day's journey) because we could not afford air tickets! We planned meticulously, rehearsed the bid questions over and over again. We set up a mock process in our offices, and got a team to act as the adjudicators, and ask questions. We practiced and practiced and practiced for two solid weeks.

When the day came, we appeared before a panel of adjudicators made up of Botswana government officials and telecoms experts from Sweden. The meeting was chaired by a leading Botswana lawyer called Mr. Moses Lekaukau, a huge man with a thundering no-nonsense style. I began my pitch by greeting the chairman in Setswana, their mother tongue. I then went into my pitch. I can still remember some of the data that I used on Botswana's demographics, its economic growth, and the market potential... numbers! After my initial pitch, they began to grill us on our presentation which was more than 900 pages: "On this page, you say that... Please explain, and what is the source of your data?" My team and I knew that document like the back of our hands, and we enjoyed each question. The grilling lasted the whole day.

A few weeks later the Botswana government announced the winner was Mascom Wireless and France Telecom (Orange) had come in second! It's is now 21 years since that "pitch." We went on to set up Botswana's and our own first telecoms business, which remains to this day the country's number one operator. No experience; Facing global competitors; No money. I was also black. (In the minds of most people at that time, there was no such thing as a serious black entrepreneur). Never allow yourself to become a "grasshopper in your own eyes," even if others see you as nothing more than a grasshopper.Since then, I've pitched to some of the greatest investors in the world, and global leaders including in 2012 to the G-8 leaders. My greatest pitch though at a personal level was this one in 1997 in Gaborone, Botswana. I will forever be grateful to the government and the people of Botswana for the opportunity.

Lessons from Strive Masiyiwa

- *Identify a need* - a problem many experience, and come up with solutions to meet the need. The problem has to be big, solvable and have great impact to the target – customers, community or country.

- *Believe in yourself* - never give up. He challenges himself to try and solve problems in Africa. He is an example that shows the court systems can work. Disrupt the status quo to make any meaningful impact on people's lives.

- *Good education:* This is a foundation that can help solve problems in Africa. He runs a foundation that educates and takes care of orphans so far over 100,000 students have benefitted from his philanthropy.

- *Evidence based decisions:* Mr. Masiyiwa depends on research that is grounded to make investments and philanthropic decisions. This is why he is a respected board member of Rockefeller foundation; he is the Chairman of AGRA (Africa Green Revolution Alliance) among other boards. He mobilized funds to fight Ebola under

African Union- this is proof that he is a respected philanthropist.

- *God* the Almighty is a good partner in your plans. Mr. Masiyiwa is known for his strong believe in prayer. He says "God will do nothing except when you pray; you have to be clear what you want". Mr. Masiyiwa is a strong advocate for the rule of law and is leading the fight against corruption in Africa.

The next story is about another great son of Africa who used alternative education- apprenticeship to success.

Cletus Ibeto: from apprenticeship to Dollar Billionaire

There is always something new or different to learn from the rich African history. Stories are told of blacksmiths, traditional doctors, rain makers and the list is endless. When formal education came to Africa it was embraced, through the formal education we have doctors, engineers, architects, lawyers and many professional careers.

Billionaire Cletus Mmadubungwa Ibeto's journey of entrepreneurship is truly intriguing and demonstrates that any route with persistence and determination will create success. It is said sometimes the ignored rock may form the foundation of a big building. There is an African saying that states 'do not put all your eggs in one basket'. Ibeto's father practised this saying in spirit, deed and action. He took his two sons to acquire formal education and sent Cletus Ibeto to his Uncle to become an apprentice. From an apprentice to $ 3.7 Billion net worth is significant. Wealth flows to anyone who has the capacity to attract it.

Early Life

Cletus was born in 1952 in Nnewi, in Anambra state in Nigeria. Nnewi is one of the industrial towns in Africa, a powerhouse in manufacturing. Ibeto's father wanted his son to be a trader. He sent him to his uncle (Charles Akamelu) in full school uniform earning the young Ibeto "school boy' tag when he was only 13 years old. His protests didn't bear any fruits. He tried hunger strike and committing suicide but he was unsuccessful. Deciding to flow with the tide, he learnt the most, kept discipline, practiced brilliance and came out a master trader. He was always the man to beat in the market. At 17 years, he was conscripted into the army during the Biafra war, a short trip to get food rations saved his engagement in the war. He escaped to go trade; what he did best.

Capital

This is normally a good excuse to many for not starting a business. Billionaire Ibeto started with what he had, a leather bag given to him by his elder brother, a round necked suit and APC tablets issued to him from an hospital is what he sold to get seed capital.

He traded and re-invested his profits in his business. His uncle was a mechanic, later a driver as well as an investor in luxury buses transport. Young Ibeto was introduced to motor vehicle spare parts, repairs and trading.

Success in Business

"Opportunity waits for no King" with his prowess in trading, he learnt that one does not need an import license to import car spare parts since the government was keen on supporting local entrepreneurs. He took the opportunity to import 65 containers of motor vehicle spare parts.

Shortly after, the government realized that the Forex reserves were dwindling and imposed an import license requirement. With his stocks, he made a lot of money due to shortage created with change of government policy. He made £4 million in just four days. The margins were very good. He managed to acquire an importation license at a price of 3 million Naira; with the liquidity he had. It was a sellers' market you dominate when it's almost a monopoly.

Transition from Trading, Importing to Manufacturing

It is always prudent to have a vision for your business. In 1988, Billionaire Ibeto started manufacturing automotive lead batteries and plastic motor vehicle parts. Initially there were local and foreign companies in battery manufacturing. With time, many closed - he is still in business. In 1995 after investing in training local Nigerians in Taiwan and having Taiwanese engineers in Nnewi for knowledge and technology transfer, he ventured into motor vehicle spare parts manufacturing which he exported to the West African region. In 1996, he invested in Petrochemicals where lubricants are manufactured as well as facilities for bulk petroleum products storage.

With changes in government policy, when one is always ready to take challenges, immense opportunities arise. He invested in cement manufacturing and bagging. He has continued to invest in other sectors of the economy namely real estate, financial services, and hospitality industry and is known to be supportive of entrepreneurs.

Mentoring others and being approachable is a source of information channel. Opportunities will seek you as you wait provided you are ready to exploit the identified opportunities to success. Nnewi today is a manufacturing hub for motor vehicle spare parts, consumables as well as utilities.

Lessons from Cletus Ibeto

- *Big Vision*: Having a purpose in life, prudently using what life throws at you. He believes in building Nigeria. He has been practical in this by investing in training local talent abroad for local placement.

- *Networks*: From trading to manufacturing, you require support of business partners. We need to invest in long term relationship. He bought used machinery to start-up his debut in manufacturing with support of partners engineers and training for his local staff. Thirty years down the line, his early workers have sons and daughters who are doctors, engineers and lawyers among other professionals.

- *Limitations are in our minds*: Breaking limitation is everyone's responsibility. If it can be made in Taiwan, we are not compelled to be forever consumers, we can move to manufacturing thus creating jobs for our people. You can always train the needed manpower in advance to align with your vision.

- *Continuous learning*: Billionaire Ibeto urges that once one is successful, you will always learn of new opportunities form people coming to you. We need to tap into this social capital always as we empower others.

- *Honesty*: To succeed in entrepreneurship one needs to be strong willed, open minded, hard -working and honest. In his local language '*Omekannya*' is a title that refers to one who acts like his father, a virtue. We need this reference when we purpose to do good always.

Note: When I was researching for my PhD thesis, I was surprised to discover that there was a village in Nigeria that had embraced manufacturing of motor vehicle parts. That village is Nnewi, now an industrial City. We can build Africa.

There's something liberating about not pretending. Dare to embarrass yourself. Risk

Drew Barrymore (American Author, Model and producer)

#9: From Fear to Faith

Many great ideas have been lost because the people who had them could not stand being laughed at. –Unknown

Fear and faith are two strange bedfellows. They are powerful motivators to action or inaction. Depending on which trigger one responds to, either procrastinates, flee or fight. Fear is an acronym of *"False Evidence Appearing Real"*. It can be captivating, enslaving and heart breaking. A few people manage to successfully confront their fear by turning onto their faith and achieving extraordinary results. Look at life with a possibility approach rather than focusing on the challenges.

One never knows what the world holds for him or her. Life sometimes can be a boring repetition. When you find yourself struggling to go to work, finding the energy to execute projects know it's time to change gears.

Phyllis W. is an advocate of the high court. Her life journey is one of determination through initially crippled by fear. She schooled in Nairobi starting in nursery school in Kibera, later joined Moi avenue primary school before ending up at Moi girls high school for her secondary school. After her "A" levels she got employed in

the banking industry, courtesy of her father
who was a banker then. She was actually
meant to join Baraton University, due to
unforeseen circumstances she ended up a
banker.

Banks offer wonderful training
opportunities through their on-job training
programmes. Working in a bank is a
prestigious employment opportunity due to
the many opportunities for personal and
career development. She worked with the
first bank for 5 years having worked as a
teller, customer care, bank operations and
recovery among other departments. She
joined a second tier bank in the credit
reporting and legal work.

Having worked in the banking industry for
10 years and seeing the work routine, she
decided to study law with the career
objective of practicing as a lawyer - her
dream career. She joined Moi University in
2001. This was a bold decision since the
banks had favourable credit facilities for
employees thereby a comfort zone. The
same year she joined Moi University she
lost her dad, a strong pillar and mentor in

her life. After law school while waiting to be admitted to the bar, she noticed she had some spare time. She enrolled for a diploma in project management since there was no quorum for Certified Public Secretary (CPS) or Non-Governmental Organizations (NGO) classes.

Studying and working are strange bedfellows; add running a family and you never have time for yourself. Studying means; attending lectures, taking assignments and frequently visiting the library for research. Changing residence from Bungoma to Eldoret also had its own challenges. Imagine leaving a relatively warm environment and getting yourself into a 'fridge'. Eldoret being in the rift valley can be really cold. Working 8am to 5pm and running to class from 5.30- 830 pm became a routine. Group work in terms of discussion groups can be very helpful in studying when time is limited. Researching and educating each other and practicing past papers can be a great relief in catching up with academia.

Work experience especially in areas one decides to further their studies always came in handy. In the bank there are a lot of legal documents prepared on daily basis. Contracts, securities perfection and execution were part of the practical aspects of law that Phyllis was already experienced in. The legal background made Phyllis really enjoy her work and the studies. She graduated in 2005 and came to Nairobi. She joined law school for her pupillage in 2007. She was admitted to the bar as an Advocate in 2008; meanwhile she continued to work under the company secretary.

In 2011, she was seconded to Kenya Bankers Association set up Kenya Credit Information Sharing Initiative (KCISI) - credit reporting and information sharing project for two years as an assistant manager in a team that dealt with project management, dispute resolution, consumer protection and financial literacy. She re-joined the bank in 2012. She worked under the company secretary handling legal and remedial unit that required banking and legal experience. She assisted clients in bad books with the bank have a soft landing without incurring hefty legal costs.

Out of court settlements enables the banks to collect bad debts and maintain better customer relations. Some cases already in court upon agreement with the customers were recalled. This was a relief to many clients. Law can be ruthless ending up with one being auctioned. Negotiating out of court settlement with a repayment plan can save a client's face. She would write to the lawyers and the board of the bank that settlement was done and a certificate issued.

Back to the bank she instituted credit information sharing unit, dispute resolution and networking among the bank branched and was actively involved in training bank staff. Part-timing as a lawyer and working in the bank was impractical. Banking work is too demanding. She even considered studying organizational development in 2013. This would help her offer team training and organizational dynamics training. She is an avid reader.

Sometimes in life there are fires that will never go away. It is called passion and desire. In 2014, the bank where she had worked for 19 strong years was retrenching. Her name was not on the list. She decided it was time to follow her passion. She requested the bank to include her name on the list of those to be retrenched. She was advised to keep off the banks, old relationships and associations that would dampen her spirit if she wanted to succeed.

She registered her law firm in 2014. She decided to tend to her family for one year before operationalizing her firm. In her first office she had problems with the rental unit. It had leaking roofs and wet peeling paint that filled the room; it was a health hazard. She had to relocate to work from home for six months before she acquired the current office address. Dampness and smell of wet paint can really be a nuisance. Personalized services are run on image. What your clients see is very important.

In her current office she deals with arbitration, mediation, out of court settlement as a consultant and legal petitioner. She serves at many committees at the Chartered Institute of Arbitrators - an option away from the courts. It saves time and is more efficient. She now happily runs two companies, her law firm and a training consultancy outfit. She believes in integrity, prayer and is self-driven. She wonders why she stayed in the bank for that long while investment and serving opportunities were there waiting for her. She now works at her pace, networks, meets people and is happy to serve.

She is currently a mediator and arbitrator, dispute resolution expert both as a practicing advocate and a consultant. She has attended several international conferences and the sky is just her starting point.

Lessons from Phyllis

- Power of negotiation builds lifelong relationships even in face of irreconcilable disputes.
- Invest in building unique skills that are in high demand on top of your professional training.

#10: From Misfit to Must-Invite

The first step toward success is taken when you refuse to be a captive of the environment in which you first find yourself. –Mark Caine

Your background has no basis in regard to the future you want. The life of Bheki Kunene, a South African, reads like a movie. It will not be long before the Nigerian movie industry picks this story of resilience and tenacity. I am almost sure the film theatres of Calabar, Abuja and Lagos will love this story of persistence and never giving up, a mantra our Nigerian brothers and sisters have perfected. Bheki was born in an environment where poverty and crime are conjoined twins. This is the same story we hear of persons born in the slums and humble backgrounds as reasons why they cannot become successful, an answer why they cannot try anything, no action means more poverty and more crime.

Mr. Bheki Kunene is a young man featured in Africa's 30 under 30 by Africa Forbes magazine. This is a great achievement for a person expelled from all government schools for hitting a teacher with a hummer - any feat of anger can bring problems to anyone. He was born in a Township in Cape Town called Gugulethu. Majority of people here are disadvantaged economically as anywhere else in the world.

Crime levels are very high. This township is remembered for two major story items; one of a couple on honeymoon from the UK, the wife was murdered and the husband is now fighting extradition and the success of Bheki Kunene. These two stories have made the world discover Gugulethu.

From Adversity to Social and Business Success

Having been expelled from school, none of the private schools would take Bheki Kunene in. He was branded a misfit, criminal, a failure; a person who belongs to the jails or the grave. How can a society be so inhumane?

All efforts to get schooling were rebuffed and resisted. He got himself in trouble with the law a couple of times; spending time in probation correctional facilities. He then got one chance of schooling and he managed to sit for his metric examinations (Equivalent of Form Four examinations, KCSE). The one chance he got to pursue education was a matter of life and death. How many of us let opportunities just pass with the notion that other better opportunities will come? Dear reader the word "poor" in essence is *passing over opportunities repeatedly*. I submit to you, you only need one chance to change your life.

After his metric examinations, he applied for a scholarship to study web and graphic design at Ruth Prowse School on condition that if he excelled in his studies his fees would be paid in full. Sometimes what people who are disadvantaged want, is just that one chance. Bheki took this golden chance and run with it. He became the best he could be.

Upon completion he was required to attend internship and he couldn't get a chance anywhere based on his past history. He decided to start a business of Web and graphic design – MINDTRIX was founded to solve his problem of internship.

His goal was to be able to graduate. In 2009, he started with $46 (KES 4800) and a computer in his bedroom. You always start with what you have to solve a problem which you get paid for. He had one happy client that kept his business going. Upon graduation, he planned to close the business and kick out the single client. When you get serious the world re-organizes itself to support your dream. The single client opened doors for MindTrix introducing Bheki Kunene to other businesses requiring his Web design and graphics design services.

Why he succeeded

His Agony: The difficulties he was experiencing became the fuel driving his persistence wanting to prove his teachers, wardens, everyone and the system that doubted him wrong. Nido Qubein says ably that "Your current status does not describe where you are going; it only states where you start." His success is the revenge to those who deemed him a misfit; a failure. Bheki did it so can you!

Passion: He was gifted in Web design and graphics that he did it with all his energy. He managed to keep his one client happy. This was the seed that brought in more clients from greater South Africa, Angola, Italy, Vietnam and USA. Follow your passion with all your might, energy and resources you can marshal. Individuals who have become successful are doing what they like which to many seem like work. To them it is like having fish in water - no struggle.

Philanthropy: Having been brought up in the neighbourhood of crime and poverty, this became his base (location) where he stationed his business to be an example to others that they too can also make it in life. He has employed 8 persons. He started a Web design and graphics school to train youths from Gugulethu Township. He has changed the lives of over 40 people. There is a connection in giving and receiving. The more you give unconditionally to make humanity better you receive in multiplied portions.

Role Model: He follows Richard Branson as his model, he had a chance to spend two days with the billionaire and that changed his life and belief system. Who thought that a "misfit" could meet the world's known billionaire who owns and runs over 300 successful enterprises in the world?

Visualization and Idealization: Thinking of the end and working backwards to build the success you want. He advises on one's need to live a balanced life. Success to him means being able to design your life. Live a life of abundance, health and relationship.

Nuggets for success

Life balance: There is no need to own the whole world and have poor health. Success is meaningful when accompanied with abundance, healthy relationships and good health.

Legacy project - Thinking about one's purpose in life is a strong motivator to actually do more to make a significant contribution to humanity. He created eight jobs, started a Web design and graphics school. He employed some of the graduates. This is a real achievement for a person branded a 'murderer' by mistake and a criminal; a misfit. Mr. Kunene has killed no one ever. A person many had given up on.

Attracting positive vibes: The mother and grandmother always encouraged him. Despite being arrested and locked up for murder then released for wrongful detention, suffering a serious road accident ending up with a broken skull. He believed in self and his mothers' vibe "So long as you are breathing there is hope."

Thoughts: Look at where you are going; not what you have experienced. What do you have to do that is required? Action brings success. Small actions collectively will change our continent Africa.

Success attracts fans: Bheki Kunene has won many accolades including getting "Youth recognition Award" by Stellenbosch University Africa Centre and being a participant in Creativity and entrepreneurship thought summit in Israel among many others.

Looking at the life and success of Bheki Kunene, we have no excuse not to succeed and contribute to the development of Africa.

Lessons from Bheki

- Take your chance and exploit the one opportunity you get as if it is the last one.
- Lift others up; it is not a sign of weakness. Mentor and grow them.
- Never give up, if you can't get, create it.

#11: *From Abundance to Nothing to Plenty*

If you're going to be thinking anything, you might as well think big. –Donald Trump

Angela was born in Rwanda. She went to school in Kigali for both primary and secondary school. The secondary school she attended was called *"Lycee Notre Dame de Citeaux"*, the equivalent of Alliance girls in Kenya. She then attended Université Nationale du Rwanda graduating with a degree in African Languages and Literature. Her life goal was to become a journalist.

During her university studies, she got a temporary job with a French firm running projects in the agricultural sector as a secretary. She worked for one year before she resumed her studies. Her professionalism made her to be recalled to work for the same firm in the same capacity. She worked for another one year before another opportunity came her way.

She got an opportunity to work for a World Bank project in Rwanda as a Personal Assistant to the National Director. This was in 1993. She was over - qualified for the job. When the genocide occurred in Rwanda she had to flee with her family to the Democratic Republic of Congo. The job disappeared since most international organizations vacated Rwanda. She returned to Rwanda after one month and was employed by the UNHCR. She worked at UNHCR for two years as a Finance and Administration Assistant. She was in-charge of South Western Rwanda near the border with DR Congo, Bukavu.

Rwanda was unstable for some time. Angela, together with her family, decided to leave in 1996 June. The family came to Kenya to no job, no relatives and no money. The previous good life in Rwanda was gone.

Picking the pieces

Always look for opportunities where you are. You will be surprised with the network you can create for your own breakthrough. When tragedy strikes, people are forced to focus on the most critical; being alive. To be alive, you need to have food and be safe. Now in Kenya with no relatives, no income she was forced to keep looking for opportunities you can give value and people can appreciate by paying.

One day, a friend shared with Angela's husband, Mr. Ephrem, that an expatriate whose children were going to a French school needed a home tutor for them. The husband got a temporary self- employment offering school children tuition services. It turned out that the parent who offered the job to Mr. Ephrem was offering translation services.

Mr. Ephrem informed her that he was a professional translator and a conference interpreter and that he could work in English and French. When a vacancy for translation and interpretation services came up, the lady gave him the information. He applied and got the job. With now a steady income, one cannot imagine the frequent change of residence from Kawangware slums to Donholm in Eastlands. Compare that with a three bedroomed bungalow back home and you feel lost.

From Donholm the family moved to Golf Course, South B, Ngummo and eventually Lavington. In one instance they were forced to change residence because of persistent water problems. Water cost was approaching 10-20% of the rent amount. In other cases, change of residence was due to children schooling, wanting to be near the school to overcome Nairobi traffic. People will never appreciate the challenges one is undergoing. Landlords in some cases want to maximize returns. Occasionally, a landlord will find that rents have gone up and they were either undercharging or they didn't know the rental value of their property. Angela found her rent increased from 50,000 shillings to 70,000 with a months' notice! She had to move out.

Meanwhile Angela's job applications were met with regrets. She has a file full of regret letters. Feeling depressed and almost giving up, a friend asked her to read a book called *'What Colour is Your Parachute?'* by Richard N. Bolles. The condition was that she had to buy her own copy. She saved and bought the book for 4000 shillings. There was a mind-set transformation towards purpose. She was reminded of her talents, passions and dreams. She remembered she wanted to be a journalist. She invested in a creative writing course offered by The Writers Bureau from Manchester, UK. She started writing stories and articles for national and international magazines. Some would be published and other articles pirated by some unscrupulous writers.

Later she tried a multi-level marketing business and though it didn't work for her, she walked away with precious knowledge and skills in sales and marketing. Through this opportunity, she got exposed to books such as *'Rich Dad, Poor Dad'* by Robert Kiyosaki and *'The E-Myth Revisited'* by Michael E. Gerber; which awakened in her the passion of empowering women economically and made her realize that for one to achieve their life objectives one needs to work with others; and not just in network marketing. This is when the idea of running her magazine was born.

She looked for space selling opportunities for leading magazines. She networked and built a portfolio of potential clients and friends. She used the skills she learnt from network marketing, reading books and watching video's to improve her skills.

Research she conducted when she wanted to start her magazine showed her that she needed 10 million shillings, enough capital to cover 24 months before advertisers would take her seriously. Anyway, she started with freelance writers and building advertisement income. She markets her magazine online and through social media apart from having a physical magazine distributed free to potential and target clients. Cost of production and operations are covered through advertisements.

Before following her heart, she opened a house helps training agency with a friend. It was a good service; the only challenge was that few employers wanted to invest in their employees' training while most employees were not committed since they didn't regard their job highly. After 6 years training house helps, they closed the business. It pays to discover what is not working when you have given your best and move on.

Today building her magazine targeting business people and mentoring start-ups resonate well with Angela. The children are now grown up, actually university graduates. The journey was tough and still is, but she never gave up. Follow your passion; you can never lie to yourself.

Lessons from Angela

- Life has ups and downs, don't stay down; you are meant to • shine like the stars.
- You can't give up - it is not an option.

You can't outwit fate by trying to stand on the side-lines and place little side bets about the outcome of life. Either you wade in and risk everything to play the game, or you don't play at all. And if you don't play, you can't win.

Judith McNaught (American Author and Radio Producer)

#12: From Job to Blank to Progress

If you don't build your dream, someone else will hire you to help them build theirs. -Dhirubhai Ambani

Mr. Johannes is one of the less than a million graduates that we have in Kenya since independence to date. He started his early schooling in Muranga where he attended primary school as well as secondary school. He attended a national school in Muranga for his "A" levels proceeding to The University of Nairobi for a degree in Bachelor of Commerce specializing in Marketing.

Upon graduation, he was employed by a Multinational Corporation (MNC) dealing in fast moving household goods (FMCG) as a customer services officer in the last quarter of 1990. He was a committed employee bagging several promotions in the same department dealing with distribution ensuring customers' orders were duly filled and served. He worked at this corporation for 5 years. The Multinational Corporation was a market leader, solid company with a reputation to boot. No one could imagine anything happening to this business empire. Employees were well taken care off. Company transport was offered to employees. Johannes was among the few who could be picked and dropped by a company van. It was a prestigious job.

In 1993, effects of competition and globalization started to take a toll on the Multinational Corporation. Local competition emerged from small outfits more agile and innovative. The era of plastic packaging took route. The MNC had deep roots in safety and global environmental standards. Their history and practice could not fathom packaging in plastics then. Their brands were market leaders' product names most of the time used generically although the customer is referring to competitors' products.

The company struggled with business improvement process, total quality control and customer focus for a while as the market was taking a hit. Then one morning the operations at the distribution department were stopped and all employees were asked to assemble in the meeting room. The meeting had been called by the customer service director. All the 50 plus employees assembled in the meeting room to find a soda and biscuits being served - this only happened during trainings. This was unusual. The temporary casual staffs were asked to wait outside the gate.

The employees were informed that the company had decided to concentrate on its core business and would outsource distribution to an international MNC with expertise in distribution to improve efficiency and cut costs. The distribution and logistics company was represented by two agents who gave a presentation of their company. They showed their equipments, warehouses and operations flow. It distributed for major MNC companies from BAT, EABL and many others. They had capacity and the efficiency required. The distribution company was founded by two friends a few years back. One of the founders had been a driver and the other a turn-boy.

The human resources manager was then invited to give a presentation on the way forward. Several options were presented namely Voluntary Severance Scheme (VSS), early retirement, options of joining the contracted distribution company or staying with the MNC although there was no guarantee of similar positions or perks as they were.

Joining Contracted distributor

The MNC distribution operations moved to Industrial area and Johannes had a new employer. The new employer was small, aggressive and efficient. Their goal was to be the leader in distribution and logistics of all major multi-national corporations. He worked from 1996 to 2001 when he decided to leave. The boss called him for a meeting earlier. The meeting discussed Johannes abilities, skills and how he could use them to better himself. The director was planning to leave and he didn't want to leave Johannes. Johannes' mind opened after the meeting. He was made aware that he could run a clearing and forwarding company, manage a warehouse, manage staff and actually run a company of his own that would be more fulfilling. Johannes was made to believe he could do better. He stopped looking at the comfort of medical cover, a good salary and a company car!

Life has more to offer to the brave who take action. He read a book *"Magic of Thinking Big"* by David J. Schwartz and felt sufficiently challenged. He asked himself why he had stayed on for that long. A few days later he saw an advert by an international humanitarian organization. He applied, was interviewed and employed. He was surprised to have doubled his salary with the new opportunity. He was promoted severally ending up as the head of warehousing. The distribution company was a great place to work in. One was exposed to different clientele to build lifelong networks. Business was plentiful since there were several accounts to service. The team was sufficiently motivated.

New skills

He trained in emergency procurement for humanitarian situations. He worked in Ethiopia during the great famine co-ordination relief food from Djibouti into Ethiopia. This was covered with the late international photo journalist Mohammed Amin. Johannes also worked in Darfur, helping set up camps and emergency supplies during the civil war.

All was well for several years. After a while, usual company politics started taking a toll on Mr. Johannes. The organization lost an employee. Interviews were conducted and one of the employees was promoted. The other colleagues were not happy and started sabotaging the organization. When your juniors start reporting to your boss without involving you - there is a problem especially if your boss is an expatriate. In such situations, believe in professionalism and fairness at all time. Johannes felt in conflict with self, there was no fulfilment in an atmosphere of insubordination.

As you work at being the best other interested parties will see and they will want to be associated with you. A friend Johannes had known for many years had grown his truck fleets from 3 to over 30 and was having problems managing. Mr. Aboud called Johannes and offered to pay him more than he was earning at the distribution company. For one to believe in you this much, your skills and expertise must be above the bar. Normally it is the *"things that we fear that cause one to grow"*.

Johannes advises, we need to be expectant in our approach to life. Having an open mind enables us see opportunities that we can exploit.

Baptism by fire

His skills were global, his practice the best and in demand. He successfully brought efficiency into the organization. On reporting, he was informed he was going for a meeting with an international MNC dealing in petroleum and petroleum products. The other colleagues at the new employer refused to accompany him. He didn't know why until he was at the meeting venue.

The operations manager complained of delayed email responses; some taking even over one month. The agency he was representing was not serious and the MNC was considering looking for other options. This was a tough business for the first encounter. Johannes asked to be orientated and possibly mentored since he was willing to learn. The engineer who was the operations manager commented he doesn't have time to waste. Being humble is a powerful virtue. The manager agreed to mentor Johannes once a month and it was Johannes responsibility to look for the operations manager. During their first mentoring meeting - Johannes was chased away by the operations manager since he had no notebook. After a few minutes he was offered a writing pad and instructed to get a good quality writing notebook if he valued the mentoring sessions. The operations manager became a father figure to Johannes who learned a lot and really improved. Johannes managed to build the business from 120,000$ a month to 500,000$ worth of business and he was given a car. He reached the pick of $1.2 million managing over 90 trucks on the road.

In 2012 Johannes decided to leave Aboud. There were internal issues with the distributor making loading of petroleum products hectic and shaky. Revenues were affected. He left to join an international logistics company in Uganda. He was interviewed and employed to meet one of his former directors who was busy looking for Johannes and could not trace him. He was interviewed via phone from South Africa and engaged. They were supplying an independent power producer with petroleum products. All was well until donor funding started reducing. For three months there were no deliveries.

Mr. Johannes re-joined Aboud in 2014. Mr. Aboud was experiencing operational and safety issues that threatened the business. Normally during audits, a contracted supplier is audited and graded. Aboud firm was graded Orange - meaning he had been given three months to improve or be terminated. Mr. Johannes developed a team that saw Aboud firm get an audit score of yellow to continue in business. This gave Mr. Aboud some space to continue investing in safety systems to enable him acquire complaint safety standards of excellence according to industry specifications – colour green.

Mr. Johannes wanted to work for self. He left Aboud in August 2015 to be able to spend quality time with his family and enjoy the flexibility of pursuing other hobbies.

Lessons from Johannes

- Build your experience and skills as you work, it's the only benefit of working for someone else.
- Build dependable networks that you can use in future.

$13: From Employment to Confusion

Do not judge me by my success, judge me by how many times I fell down and got back up again- Nelson Mandela

Tsheena Anyanga's early life started in western Kenya. She started her primary school in Kakamega. She was a bright girl. She was close to an Aunt who was partially blind. The Aunt had a desktop computer that helped her with reading. It is this desktop computer that enabled Tsheena Anyanga, learn how to read before children her age. This encounter saw Tsheena skipping three classes (standard one to three). She could read very well; her only challenge was comprehension. She started school in standard four third term. She struggled with science and mathematics.

Skipping classes for bright children has its advantages and disadvantages. The advantage is finishing early schooling before the scheduled time. The disadvantage is one is forced to grow faster through interaction with children their senior. In secondary, she schooled near her home in Nyanza. She passed secondary school examination well. Tsheena had a dream of being an air hostess. Using mock results she applied for a college in Nairobi for tours and travel.

The village is a unique place, most careers are very predictable. In the village one is either a teacher, civil servant or a nurse. Tsheena Anyanga application for college was accepted. She discussed with her parents to be able to attend college. Going to university was not in the cards for Tsheena Anyanga.

She travelled to Nairobi to stay with an Aunt. She was given a car and a driver to make her stay comfortable. She got bored and wanted more freedom. She approached Young Women Christian Association (YWCA) hostel for a quotation which she took to her parents. This was in 2000. She passed the IATA course very well and applied to join an international airline as an air hostess. While waiting, she worked with an airline as part of the ground crew.

The dream to be an air hostess did not materialize. She incorporated modelling in her career as well as she continued learning. She joined Kenya Institute of Management to study Diploma in Management involving accounts and human resources management. She joined a leading hospital as a human resource officer. She didn't report to work for three months since she was comfortable from payments of modelling engagements.

She later joined the organization and the salary was disheartening. She decided to continue improving her skills in order to earn a promotion. She enrolled in the Kenya Railway Institute for a higher Diploma in Management. Promotions in the civil service were frozen in 2000 at some point in the past. Staring as a clerk she grew in rank ending up as a senior clerk in 2009. She bagged various awards as a committed and reliable employee severally.

Her shinning role caused her transfer to the finance department which she didn't want. Her modelling work improved her wardrobe. She had a taste for fashion to the dislike of her colleagues. She was dressing above her rank and had a chauffeur driven car provided by a relative. We need to learn to appreciate our colleagues at work. Everyone needs to compete with their potential and opportunities they can attract. We cannot be the same in this life irrespective of our levels of income. She resisted moving to the finance department since she hated finance.

In life what we dislike may be the opportunity we need to excel. She finally gave up and decided to be the best employee she had always been. She started selling children clothes on the side to fellow workers making tidy sums on money.

Problems started when colleagues thought she was using the organizations' money to finance her stylish lifestyle. She would be harassed with unexpected audits. She was, however, a committed and honest worker.

In finance, money can be tempting. At one time a colleague was using her phone to reply to a friend who was asking for a soft loan. Unknown to her, the text message went to the director saying, "Sorry I cannot loan you since I have an unofficial loan amounting to almost millions." As Murphy's Law states, what will go wrong will go wrong.

A crisis was in the offing. Within three hours, teams of people were auditing all cash handling offices. Audits and investigations were carried out. A little discrepancy meant interdiction or suspension. 60% of the accounts staff had matters to answer.

Expecting a baby, this was unnecessary stress. She was confident she could survive without a job. Tsheena Anyanga decided she didn't want her job back.

Anyone without a job finds themselves with a lot of free time at their disposal. Without a plan, then you add a fat bank account the result is a disaster. Idleness loves company and gossip. Not long after Tsheena Anyanga would find herself in the malls in the company of house wives sipping coffee, imbibing alcohol and her life changed.

Her children missed her. She was a stranger to them. Alcohol and bad company are the worst enemies of development. This continued for a while as her bank account was being drained day by day.

Social media could not come at a good time. She came across a mentorship programme by Dr. Kinyanjui when she felt she wanted something different in life. She started attending the mentorship sessions and slowly getting organized in life. She started going to church, took classes and was baptized signalling a new beginning.

Mentorship is a powerful tool in re-shaping one's destiny. She has changed her associations. Her children enjoy her company. She is now more focused on personal development. She continued enrolling for educational courses graduating from a private university. Today she runs an events management company and a mentoring company. The sky is the limit. She is happier and more fulfilled. Tsheena is a proud member of Sense 101.

Lessons from Tsheena

- You can always have a brand new start; all you need to do is decide.
- Choose your associations; they have a great influence on you by choice or default.
- Family is important for your peace and happiness.

> *I learned that courage was not the absence of
> fear, but the triumph over it. The brave man
> is not he who does not feel afraid, but he who
> has conquers the fear -*
>
> **Nelson Mandela (Former South African
> president and Nobel Laurent)**

#14: *From Employment to Entrepreneurship*

It always seem impossible until it is done -Nelson Mandela

Life has a way of playing jigsaw puzzles with people. What appear as hopeless situations are actually the success bricks that build immense wealth. History is full of examples of people who went through very difficult upbringing, where food was either scarce or not available at all. Mr. Cosmas Maduka, a Nigerian billionaire shared his experiences during the Biafra war where food was scarce people could not farm and majority of the population were forced to eat any leaves, insects and animals. They would experiment with one person and if nothing happened to the person, it became food. It was better to die trying to save yourself from hunger than the hunger killing you; they reasoned!

Their drive and motivation to change ones' circumstances have been strong pillars on which successful businesses have been built. The businesses have been developed to solve common problems in society. The society responds by being good patrons to the problem solver with their wallets.

Mr. Maingi was a seasoned marketer working in the once vibrant pharmaceutical industry. I admired his prowess in closing sales. He was a master salesman. He was a people's person and still is to date. He built strong customer relationships and had intelligence welded in comic. People were always happy in Maingi's company.

Maingi comes from a humble background. He was born in Machakos, attended a primary school at Makaalu, being a brilliant child, he scored 470 out of 500. He then joined Machakos Boys' in Machakos County. He later proceeded to Egerton University where he graduated with a Bachelor of Science degree in Agriculture. I have always opined that what you study in the formal education does not matter; it is just a bridge to your destiny and legacy.

His first employment was with a pharmaceutical company in Mombasa where we were colleagues. His sales star was shining. He would achieve his targets periodically until he was offered a company car. With the car his sales targets continued being raised. After about three years he got married to Everlyne in 2001. They were blessed with a daughter the same year.

His contract with the first employer came to an end. I remember him crying. I consoled my friend that it would be well. The wife was working as a clinician in Mombasa. Shortly after, Maingi got another job opportunity as a pharmaceutical sales representative still based in Mombasa. After one year with the new employer, Maingi started a uniform manufacturing outfit in Kisauni, along the old Malindi - Mombasa road. He also designed African Outfits that were very popular. He resigned a year later to become self-employed.

Your success will always come from using what you have to get what you want. Using his sales and marketing skills he managed to get business from hotels and hospitals in Mombasa and the coastal region. He had employed about 15 persons deriving livelihood from this uniform outfit. As growth beckoned, his employee numbers increased to 25. He continued the uniform business until 2012, when the competition became too fierce to manage steering the business profitably.

The beauty about enterprise is that the entrepreneur is always on the driver's seat. Always scanning the environment for opportunities and looking around for possible threats and risks to the business. The skill and ability enables one to make strategic choices for one's own survival.

Entrepreneur Maingi ventured into furniture and hardware business in 2012. He then opened a large workshop along Mtamboni road still in Kisauni area. His business designed and fabricated furniture for hotels, bars and restaurants. As a business grows, other investment opportunities crop up. There was need for fabrics. I remember talking to Maingi, a few weeks ago, he had just returned from a business trip in China. I wanted to actually meet him to find out how is China?

When I called him next, my friend was on his way to Turkey to source for fabrics. Maingi has been importing fabrics since the year 2016. His workforce at the moment is 30 persons strong. He has his eyes on the regional, national and East Africa in the years to come.

Today Maingi can farm using his agribusiness training gained at the university. Necessity is truly the mother of invention. Mr. Maingi was motivated to start a business out of his experience with the first employer. The desire to take care of his family and provide was a major driver to his success. I was joking to Maingi that he should consider working for his first employer since the seed of success was planted then. He advises he is happy the way things turned out. It made him realize his potential in life. He counsels no one is useless, find your own flow and shine.

Lessons from Entrepreneur Maingi

- Get back your economic engine - try the fastest legal means you can get to start earning some income.
- Plan your exit to your desired lifestyle - get skills, start a business, save.
- Follow your DREAM; don't wait forever.

Never Give up. Today is hard, tomorrow will be worse but the day after tomorrow will be sunshine

Jack Ma (Real name Ma Yun, Chinese Business Magnate and Founder of Alibaba group)

#15: Sacked, What Next

A mind that is stretched by a new experience can never go back to its old dimension -Oliver Vendell Homes Jr.

You can't live your life in fear. We need to have faith. It is the only powerful match and replacement of fear. Believe it can be done. Man was created a "creator"; not just a consumer. We all have the creative genes in our DNA; all that is needed is to activate it. The owner of the business you are working for; whether it is an individual, corporate or government, the job was created by someone. This means and implies that we can also create if we choose to.

If you have never been sacked, retrenched or retired - prepare yourself since you don't know the place or time it will occur. We live in an uncertain world. How do you prepare? Gain skills and experiences that you can use today and in future. Invest in savings and personal development. Build networks; they may be necessary in future. Remember we are in this world for a season, what do we want to be remembered for? You are lucky you can choose when to fire your boss. Plan, plan and plan. Then prepare, prepare and prepare. Lastly, execute your plan - it is your life.

If you ever find yourself without a job, look inside you, what skills and experiences do you have? What problems do you see in the world that you can solve? Can you be a broker? Can you work on commission, there are online jobs, and do you have the networks to engage in them? What can you do from home that people can pay for? Can you bake cakes or biscuits? Are you trustworthy and can be a source of information especially for rare information? Can you be a writer? Can you teach people some common skills in demand like how to write a CV? How to dress? How to speak? Are you good with children? Can you help working mothers with professional day care services?

The list is endless. The basis of starting a business or getting employment is based on similar premise "what problem can you solve fast and affordably?"

For you to be able to survive the "sack' you need three things namely: skills that are in demand (meaning they are scarce), secondly you need to have some track record, (some experience that is believable) and lastly as you work you need to build a network of reliable friends, suppliers and customers. You don't know which problem you will be solving in future.

Having a critical self-analysis of your situation and being real is part of facing the problem with the aim of solving it. Have a discussion with your spouse or trusted friend- for a problem shared is a problem half solved. Talking to someone you trust brings down the stress levels and may bring positive perspectives to the situation. Next try and look around your circles of friends or past colleagues who happened to experience a similar situation. Is it possible to reach out and let them share their experiences? One would be surprised that a good number of people who are sacked end up better in life than most of those who are not.

There is hope. There are many problems in Africa and Kenya that we are called upon to solve. The problems include; food, insecurity, education, health, energy, clothing, housing, fodder for animals, water and sanitation. Any problem solved with efficiency, reliability and sustainability can generate immense wealth. The middle class need repairs, entertainment, fashionable apparels, jewellery, personalized services. What can you offer?

The problem majorly is lack of innovation and not money. How else do you explain a hawker starting a business with 3000 and ending up a millionaire? An apprentice starting with no money buys out the boss. Focus on the problem you want to solve and the skills that are required.

Always start with your time, your skills and abilities and let people pay you for that as you raise your capital to invest in your desired venture.

Epilogue

This book is meant to give you, the reader, hope when you encounter a hopeless situation. In many cases of people losing their jobs by either being sacked, retrenched, retired before time, companies closing down operations, services being outsourced, it is not all negative. How do you explain why majority end up doing better in life than colleagues they left behind in employment? Are we in employment for fear of the unknown? Instead of working we are busy bodies chatting on Facebook, gossiping and just passing time.

Brothers and sisters when the time comes you need to replace the fear with faith. Those who have gone through that baptism will advise you that results come from the actions that you take. Complaining never solves anything; bitterness blinds one to new opportunities. When you find yourself in difficulties I urge you to remember only two situations. First remember Nick Vujicic who was born without limbs. He has no arms no legs and his mantra is no problem. He has a family, he writes books, and he is a gifted international speaker and preacher. What about you? God has given you all your limbs, you are healthy and there is a lot you can do, why waste precious time complaining? GET TO WORK with a renewed attitude.

Secondly, remember David and Goliath the Philistine. The Israelites were challenged. They were afraid and terrified. David got to know of the challenge; if Goliath killed his opponent the Israelites would be slaves to the Philistines. On the other hand should someone kill Goliath he was promised bounty wealth, the king's daughter and freedom from taxes for him and his family. Everybody else was afraid except David who had faith in the Lord of Israel. Success comes from common things done extraordinarily. David's brothers discouraged him - in their mind he was only fit to herd sheep. Saul gave him armour which he couldn't use since he had not practiced. Remember our discussion of 'what are your skills and experiences?' David was experienced in killing lions and bears while herding flock. He used his fling and polished shinny stones from the river.

The challenge Goliath, David did not see a giant, he saw a big target he couldn't miss. Goliath saw a young inexperienced boy fit to feed wild birds and wild animals. Instead of the sling, he saw weapons meant for a dog. David knew he didn't only have the sling; he had the Lord of Israel with him.

Dear friend, choose your Goliath and take common things and execute them extraordinarily. That is what brings and builds success. Every challenge has better fruits in the end, keep the faith.

All stories in this book are true stories of real people. Learn from their experiences and be a better person. Be the light to others. WHAT IS YOUR STORY?

Author's Profile

Vincent Ogutu is passionate about Business Success and Entrepreneurship. He is an academic researcher and author. Among his published works are: <u>Influence of investment groups in creation of SME's in Nairobi County; Impact of business incubators in economic growth and entrepreneurship development; A story "on the wing in Africa" in a children's book :*Acting for Nature*, published in the USA</u>. He has published his first book in Kenya: "*Life is Like That*". It is transformative, entertaining and mind opening. He is currently working on his third book and assisting a client write a book.

He started off as a pharmaceutical sales representative, today he is a Business Coach helping entrepreneurs improve, grow and accelerate their businesses. His areas of interest are business management, marketing, strategy and entrepreneurship development. He is currently pursuing Doctoral (PhD) studies in Entrepreneurship at JKUAT.

Vincent is a regular speaker at meetings and conferences and has mentored many entrepreneurs, trained many Sacco's and organized groups. He currently runs a Consultancy Firm with interest in growing Entrepreneurs is Small and Medium size enterprises (SME's). He is a mentor with Tony Elumelu Entrepreneurship Programme (TEEP) running entrepreneurship mentorship all over Africa. Vincent is married and lives in Nairobi with his family.

He can be reached on 0722171838
Email: vincent.ogutu@advancebizness.co.ke
or ogutuvin@gmail.com

Trainings and Seminars Offered

How to write a book and become a published Author: *This training programme is called* **becoming a Successful published Author (BAPA).** *It is a six months programme meeting every two weeks for two hours. It is practical, experiential and from which you graduate with a book in your hand.*

EMPLOYMENT TO NTREPRENUERSHIP (E2E): A Step by Step Programme to move you from Employment to Entrepreneurship. *This is a six months programme that enables one to practically transit from employment to running a successful business. It is practical and intensive. It focuses on Process and Results.*

Resources

1. Books

    - *Life is like that: Power of Life Contradictions*
    - *Sacked! So What? Power of Hope and Action*

2. eNewsletter

Subscribe to our free educative weekly newsletter "SPOTLIGHT on ENTREPRENEURSHIP AND BUSINESS SUCCESS" send an email to: *info@advancebizness.co.ke*

There Is Hope, Act And Follow Your Dream

The end of a contract is a signal to a new beginning. There is no reason to be depressed, hopeless and bitter. It is time to audit your skills, experiences and look for opportunities to serve. It is surprising that those retrenched, sacked or retired become more successful than when they were in employment.

Your future lies on your mind-set. There is time to learn what it takes, understand what is required and implement what is needed with speed, efficiency and consistency. Execute the ordinary extraordinarily.

NO EXCUSE, GET DOWN to work, with renewed ATTITUDE!

This book is about individuals who found themselves without jobs for one reason or another. They are real stories of struggle, action and triumph. Face your Goliath; learn, act and excel.

From Zero to Significance - one step at a time

From Pain to Wealth - motivation to succeed

From Employment to Entrepreneurship - journey to freedom

Vincent is an Author, inspirational speaker and trainer in entrepreneurship, personal development and wealth creation. He lectures on entrepreneurship and has mentored many entrepreneurs. He is currently pursuing his doctorate training in Entrepreneurship at JKUAT. Vincent mentors for Tony Elumelu Entrepreneurship Programme (TEEP). He is married and lives in Nairobi with his family.

* 9 7 8 9 9 6 6 1 0 7 2 0 6 *